Barraud, London

ROBERT W. BUCHANAN

Twayne's English Authors Series

Sylvia E. Bowman, *Editor*

INDIANA UNIVERSITY

Robert W. Buchanan

 157

Robert W. Buchanan

JOHN A. CASSIDY

Indiana University

Twayne Publishers, Inc.　:　:　New York

821.89
B918 C

ISBN 0-8057-1066-3

To the Memories

of Miss Elizabeth McMullen

and

Professor Finley Foster

Teachers and Beloved Friends

Preface

Though today a too-little known poet, playwright, novelist, critic, Robert Williams Buchanan is still a Victorian literary figure who must be reckoned with. In the hurly-burly of the twentieth century most students of English literature know Buchanan only as "the man who attacked Rossetti." But Buchanan's record as a humanitarian is notable. He concerned himself vitally with the problems and the life of his times; and he fought manfully against the prevailing Victorian views on prudery, censorship, war, women's rights, and socialism. Indeed, Archibald Stodart-Walker's contemporary study of him is entitled *Poet of Modern* [Victorian] *Revolt.* Although Buchanan's stand on these matters brought him into disfavor with his more orthodox contemporaries, the societal changes of the twentieth century have amply vindicated him as a man who was far ahead of his time.

Nor should he be forgotten on purely literary grounds, for he had a measure of true genius. Many of his poems, some of his novels, several of his plays, and a sprinkling of his critical essays contain both pleasure and profit for the modern reader. My aim in this book is to present Buchanan and his works in such a fashion that today's reader may gain some understanding of who he was and what he did, as well as of how he fitted into the general Victorian picture. My design has been, first, to set the man against the background of his times and to examine closely the formative influences that shaped his life and literary career. Then follows a critical examination of the works, arranged by type and genre, in order to arrive at a final estimation of his achievement and his place in Victorian literature. Finally, because he was a humanitarian and a Socialist, I have commented upon his relationship to sociological developments in his own times and in the twentieth century.

In this work I have incurred many obligations. I gratefully acknowledge my indebtedness to the late Professor Finley M. K. Foster, who first set my feet on the Buchanan trail. Mr. Robert Ashley Stevenson performed invaluable research service during an exchange teachership in Scotland and England. Professor Lyon N.

Richardson has given me both encouragement and inspiration. The British Museum and the Lord Chancellor's Office have furnished me with microfilms of manuscript materials. My colleagues, Professors Lawrence J. Clipper and Edward A. Kopper, Jr., read my manuscript and offered valuable suggestions. Mr. John S. Mayfield, Curator of Manuscripts and Rare Books, Syracuse University Library, has given me important bibliographical aid, as well as reading the manuscript and sharing with me his rich knowledge of Victoriana. To Professor Sylvia Bowman, editor of this series, I am especially obligated for wise, patient, and inspirational editorial assistance.

JOHN A. CASSIDY

Indiana University

Acknowledgments

I owe a debt of gratitude to Messrs. Chatto and Windus for permission to quote from their 1901 edition of Buchanan's *Complete Poetical Works* and to quote from his novels, plays, and books of critical essays, the copyrights of which are under their ownership.

Acknowledgment is also made to the Modern Language Association for permission to use in a different form material from my articles, "Robert Buchanan and the Fleshly Controversy," *Publications of the Modern Language Association*, March, 1952, and "The Original Source of Hardy's Dynasts," *Publications of the Modern Language Association*, December, 1954.

Contents

Chronology

1841   Robert Williams Buchanan born August 18 in Caverswall, Lancashire.

1850   Family moves to Glasgow; father editor of *Glasgow Sentinel,* Socialist newspaper.

1851   Father purchases *Sentinel* and stirs up hatred against self and family by attacks in paper upon religion and capitalism.

1855   Father purchases *Glasgow Times* and *Penny Post.*

1856   Father declared bankrupt. Young Robert enters University of Glasgow.

1857   Friendship with David Gray, also a student and an ambitious young poet. The two young men send letters seeking advice and help from British literary notables.

1860   Father's complete financial failure brings crisis. Robert and Gray to London to seek literary fortune.

1861   Robert becomes reviewer for *Athenaeum* under editorship of Hepworth Dixon. Marriage to Mary Jay. Death of Gray in December.

1862   Collaborates with Charles Gibbon on first play, *The Rathboys.* Beginning of friendship with George H. Lewes, George Eliot, and Thomas Love Peacock.

1863   Publishes first book, *Undertones,* poems on Classical themes.

1864   Friendship with Robert Browning. Awarded medal for *Undertones* by Society of Fine Arts. Failure of second play, *The Witchfinder,* causes him to leave playwriting for ten years.

1866   Death of father; mother lives in Robert's home until her death in 1894; *London Poems* one of three works that help establish reputation. With family, resides at Oban, Scotland, for eight years. Satire on Swinburne, "The Sessions of the Poets," in *Spectator.*

1869   Monetary difficulties lead him to give readings from his works in London. Physical breakdown from overwork. Granted a Civil List pension of hundred pounds a year for life.

1871   October, publishes article, "The Fleshly School of Poetry: Mr. D. G. Rossetti," in *Contemporary Review.* Causes lifelong enmities and seriously damages Buchanan's career.

1876   Completes first novel, *Shadow of the Sword.* Awarded a hundred and fifty pounds damages for Swinburne's libelous writings against him. Friendship with novelist Charles Reade. Letters to newspapers urge English financial aid to Walt Whitman.

1877   Publishes poem *Balder the Beautiful.*

1881   November, death of wife; expenses of her illness force him to hasty, careless writing to make money. Publishes novel *God and the Man* with notable apology to Dante Gabriel Rossetti for attack of 1871–72.

1882   Publishes novel of protest against journalistic scandal-mongering, *The Martyrdom of Madeline.*

1884   With Harriett Jay to United States; he meets and forms friendship with Walt Whitman.

1888   Embittered because religious epic, *City of Dream*, not well received.

1892   Death of Tennyson; Buchanan mentioned as possible poet laureate.

1893   Publishes poem *Wandering Jew*; increasing depression because it is not successful. Article in *Idler* advises young against literary career.

1894   Death of mother plunges him into despair. Unwise speculation causes bankruptcy and loss of copyrights.

1897   Publishes himself his poetic *Ballad of Mary the Mother*, savage attack upon Christianity.

1899   January, severe attack of angina followed by pneumonia leaves him an invalid.

1901   June 10, death. Burial at Southend-on-Sea with Anglican rites.

CHAPTER 1

An Owenite Victorian

WHEN Robert Williams Buchanan died on June 10, 1901, in London, the *Times* remarked in its obituary that the discontent with the world as he found it was an inheritance from his father.[1] This statement is true but not complete. Buchanan had indeed learned from his father many of the ideas and beliefs that shaped his entire life, but the father was only passing on what he had acquired from Robert Owen, social philosopher and reformer, whose disciple he was. Owen had found much wrong with the world and had spent most of his life and fortune in a vain attempt to remedy it. Owen, an optimist and a man of peace, had emphasized the remedies more than the wrongs; but disciple Buchanan had loved combat and had delighted in attacking the evils of society. This negative view of things and an aggressive temperament to go with it he bequeathed to his son.

Equally important in young Buchanan's career was the fact that much of his dissatisfaction with his Victorian environment resulted from its impact upon his essentially Victorian character. For the Victorian mind was keenly self-analytical and self-critical. The bewildering changes in the conditions of life and man's obvious inability to control his rapidly developing world filled thinking people with dread. Literary men like Thomas Carlyle, Robert Browning, John Ruskin, Algernon Swinburne, Matthew Arnold, Charles Dickens, William Thackeray, and William Morris raised their voices against current folly and stupidity; for they foresaw grave disasters unless radical changes were made. Buchanan did likewise; and his poems, novels, plays, and critical essays are filled with his dissent and admonition.

In Buchanan's case, his Owenite inheritance reinforced his Victorian conscience to render his protest more vehement than that of most of his contemporaries. This fact is not surprising, for most of Owen's dogmas involved principles which, often under other names and philosophical headings, loomed large in the Victorian world. Buchanan's fretting about religion and the existence of God, for instance, grew out of the Owenite claim that God was an out-

moded myth and that the world's religions were only hoaxes; but it
was also predicated upon Victorian doubts engendered by the
scientific theories of Erasmus and Charles Darwin, Jean Lamarck,
and Sir Charles Lyell, as well as by the religious writings of Ernest
Renan, David Friedrich Strauss, and Auguste Comte. Buchanan's
championing of the cause of fallen women as the victims of man's
lust stems from Owen's assertion that woman should be man's equal,
not his chattel, and that prostitution was a direct result of the false
sanctity given to marriage by the priesthood; but it also owes much
to the Victorian thrust for women's rights and for the rehabilitation
of fallen women that came about in the late decades of the century.

From the same mixed influences came that stubborn intolerance
of eroticism and pornography which led to Buchanan's attack upon
Dante Gabriel Rossetti and Swinburne in the Fleshly Controversy
of 1871. Similarly, Buchanan was attracted to the Positivism of
Auguste Comte because both Comte and Owen denied the validity
of religion and insisted that man could achieve an earthly utopia by
the use of reason. But Positivism was popular in the Victorian world
of the 1860's, 1870's, and 1880's; and many of Buchanan's friends
were drawn to it. Likewise, Buchanan's membership in the Humanitarian League and his opposition to vivisection, hunting, and fishing
were at least a partial reaffirmation of the Owenite doctrine that in
the New Moral World, as Owen styled his utopian vision, such a
spirit of love would prevail that cruelty to animals would cease
along with man's inhumanity to man. But Buchanan's humani-
tarianism was undeniably intensified by the Victorian ideal growing
out of Darwin's *Origin of Species* in 1859 that if man had evolved
from animals, it behooved him to be considerate of them. Finally,
Buchanan's unshakable belief in progress was both Owenite and
Victorian. His gloom in the 1890's when, like many of his contemporaries, he came to the bitter realization that man would use
science and invention for evil as well as for good was all the heavier
because his optimism had been all the more fervent.

There are other things in Buchanan, of course, and we shall deal
with them where necessary. But his Owenism and Victorianism
predominate and form the *leitmotivs* of his life and work.

I *Owenism*

In 1837 a humble journeyman tailor of Ayrshire, Scotland,
probably in his early twenties, was so strongly attracted to Owen's

startling doctrines of the New Moral World that he cast aside his needle and scissors and traveled the two hundred and fifty miles to Huddersfield, England, to do his part in expounding the new gospel.[2] Of his family and his parentage we know nothing beyond the certainty that they were poor. Some faint light is thrown upon his ancestry by his son Robert's assertion in later years:

> *From a race of cattle stealers,*
> *Rievers of the clan Buchanan*
> *I, Buchanan, sprang—the riever's*
> *Savage blood is in my veins . . . .*[3]

Robert Owen (1771–1858) was an early specimen of that breed of wealthy industrialists and businessmen, frequently seen in nineteenth-century Britain and America, who became actively interested in social reform. From humble Welsh beginnings, he rode Crompton's mule as a sort of winged horse to such a pinnacle of success that by 1800 he became superintendent and part owner of the giant textile mills at New Lanark, Scotland, near Glasgow. There he found conditions so abject among the fifteen hundred adults and five hundred poor children in his mills that he undertook a program of social improvement and education. So successful was he, at least in his own judgment, that by 1817 he urged Parliament to establish in Britain a series of communities on the general plan of his establishment at New Lanark—communities into which the poor could be gathered, twelve hundred to a community, where they could live together, work together, and be educated together. The implementation of his plan, Owen asserted, would effect such a complete regeneration of society that crime and poverty would soon vanish, and mankind would achieve something very near to utopia.

Parliament was not persuaded, and the rich, whom Owen confidently expected to provide the necessary money to get his communities started, failed to respond. In 1822, Owen took his cause to Ireland, where he again met with failure. In 1824, turning his back forever on New Lanark and his industrial career, he journeyed to the United States where he lost four-fifths of his fortune trying to establish a colony at his own expense; then to Mexico; and finally back to England in 1829. Here he was surprised and pleased to find that hard times had blighted the economy and that British workers were now quite receptive to his ideas. With alacrity Owen projected himself into the forefront of the labor movement, publishing on

November 1, 1834, the first issue of his weekly paper, *The New Moral World*, exclusively devoted to spreading his views among the working classes. In 1835, with himself as president, he announced the "Association of All Classes of All Nations," a high-sounding title covering a large group of people who were more or less convinced of the viability of his theories. So rapidly did the association grow that at its annual meeting, or congress, in 1837, most of the industrial cities of northern England were represented. To expedite the propagation of the Owenite gospel, it was voted to establish a missionary society under the direction of Owen, now given the pontifical title of Rational Social Father, and to employ paid missionaries to bear the brunt of the work.

By 1837, when Buchanan joined the movement, Owen's thinking had developed to such a degree that he considered it necessary to attack and destroy the age-old concepts of religion and the family before his new ideas could win popular acceptance. Borrowing liberally from the published works of William Godwin, Thomas Paine, and others of the more radical thinkers of the day, Owen, as early as 1817, had proclaimed that all the great religions of the world were the stultifying influence that had so enchained the mind of man in bigotry, prejudice, and superstition that he had been unable to discover or traverse the easy, natural road to the New Moral World. As set up by such religions, the concept of the family was an evil because it fostered selfishness in the private possession of property. In turn, such selfishness promoted strife, crime, and all the other evils of society. Furthermore, the family rested upon, and grew out of, the institution of matrimony as established by the old religions, an institution which forced man and woman to live in bondage to each other, even though in many cases their affection might long have vanished.

In place of religion Owen offered the sweet reasonableness of Owenism in promoting a world of peace and harmony in which all would work together, would hold all wealth and goods in common, and would develop mutual tolerance and affection. Without the rivalries, strife, and hatred engendered by greed, he argued, such a happy state of society should be easily attainable, especially if aided by education and the power of human reason. Much later, in 1835, he expressed his conviction that this upward progress might be assisted by the forces of nature controlled by a Power or Existence that dominated the universe, governing it by laws and principles beyond man's comprehension, and unmoved by man's wishes and prayers, a vague bit of Deism that was as close as Owen ever came to admitting the existence of God.

To eliminate the evils of the family, Owen proposed to reduce marriage to the level of a social contract between man and woman, one formed simply by agreement between them and dissolved in the same fashion. To eradicate other injustices, he proposed to give woman equal rights and education with man and to establish her as man's social companion, not in any sense as his chattel. Any training of the children in the home was to be reduced to an absolute minimum to prevent their absorption of selfish ideas of family importance or of family ownership of property. At the age of three, children were to enter into the community schools where they would be thoroughly grounded in Owenite doctrines, would be treated always with kindness and sympathy, and would be taught to accept their schoolmates as brothers and sisters and to treat them as such.[4]

This, then, was the cause young Buchanan joined in 1837. His native shrewdness, zeal, and natural eloquence enabled him to rise so rapidly that he soon became one of the ten paid missionaries; and by 1840 he was holding the important post of Social Missionary to Manchester and vicinity. His life was a busy one, and he threw himself into it with gusto. Socialist meetings were held on Sundays, when the workers were free to attend. In order to woo religious people to the Owenite cause, the pattern of the meetings was quite similar to orthodox church services. Socialist philosophy was read instead of the Bible; Socialist "hymns" were sung about the virtues of benevolence, liberty, industry, temperance, truth and wisdom. At the meetings Socialist children were named but, of course, never baptized. Since Buchanan was soon known among the Socialist following as a poet, he may well have composed some of the hymns.

Although the gentle Owen sought to avoid strife and urged his followers to do likewise, his attacks upon religion, marriage, and the family met with considerable opposition; and, from 1837 on, the angry forces of orthodoxy arose to harry and heckle him and his missionaries wherever they dared to appear. Some of the more militant, Buchanan among them, seemed to enjoy the strife, for they fanned the fires by heaping ridicule upon religion and marriage at every opportunity. Buchanan took especial delight in attempting to explode the popular belief in Satan and ghosts by producing a pseudo-ghost with a magic lantern.[5] The inevitable result was that the Socialists were soon barred from town halls and were refused permission to meet at all in some towns; in others, mob violence was used against them. Not infrequently, the missionaries were forced to flee for their lives, often depending upon the Socialist faithful to hide them and spirit them away from the rage of their foes.

Buchanan's missionary activities brought him to the hamlet of Stoke-on-Trent, where lived a professed Socialist named Attorney Williams, whose first name eludes us but who commanded such personal respect from the townspeople that he was able to save many Owenite lecturers from their ferocity. Under such circumstances, perhaps, Buchanan met and won Miss Margaret Williams, Attorney Williams's daughter. They were married in 1840 in a civil ceremony at which Owen himself gave away the bride.

As time went on, Buchanan's conduct in his career as a missionary waxed even more aggressive than it had been. The religious opposition brought forth a recently ordained Methodist minister, the Reverend John Brindley, who delighted in debating and heckling the Owenite lecturers wherever they appeared. So insulting was he and so boorish his manners on the lecture platform that the gentler Owenites could not cope with him. Buchanan took him on in several confrontations and at least held his own. As tempers mounted, the clerical party and their adherents became ever fiercer and, not content with verbal reprisals, wreaked violence upon their foes. Disaster overtook Buchanan at Whitehaven, an English west-coast town a hundred miles south of Glasgow, to which he was summoned to speak against the attacks of the Reverend Mr. Salt, the Methodist minister of the place. The Owenites rented a hall and announced that on a certain evening in January, 1842, Buchanan would lecture. But, when the evening arrived and the hall was filled, a mob appeared, broke down the hastily barred doors, smashed the furniture, beat the men who had not fled, tore the clothing from their backs, and allowed only the women to go unharmed. As the account in the *New Moral World* put it, "Buchanan ran for it; but was hunted, caught, and very roughly treated."[6] So roughly, in fact, that he was laid up for several weeks. By April, 1842, if we may judge from the reports in the *New Moral World*, his career as a missionary had concluded.

Shortly thereafter the Socialist movement bogged down because of financial troubles, which grew progressively worse with the succession of crop failures and deteriorating industrial conditions. The Owenite faithful were mostly of the working class; and, out of work as they were, they could not contribute the money to keep the cause going. Besides, Chartism, which had rapidly come to the fore, had caused many defections from the Owenite ranks. By midyear of 1842, the Owenite situation was so dire that all the missionaries had to be discharged for lack of funds. In 1845, the ambitious Owenite colony at Queenwood closed for the same reason. For all practical purposes, Robert Owen's movement was at an end.

II *Childhood to Manhood*

Robert Williams Buchanan was born at Caverswall in Lancashire, a village within a few miles of the home of lawyer Williams at Stoke-on-Trent, on August 18, 1841.[7] A sister who followed him some twelve years later died in infancy, and he was reared as an only child who was loved by his father and doted upon by his attractive mother. Indeed, the affection between the mother and son forms one of the strongest currents in his life and works. Frequently he refers to her in his poetry in loving terms; wherever he mentions motherhood in any of his novels or plays, he does so with awe and reverence; and this mother complex carries over into an idealization of womanhood so extreme that it was remarkable even in that Victorian day when such an idealization was commonplace.

The mother's influence was not altogether a good one. Inheriting his father's quick temper and dynamic disposition, Robert needed a firm hand to curb him; instead, his mother surrounded him with an excess of love, indulged his whims, and shielded him from every hard knock. The father, even had he been so inclined, could hardly have found time to take a hand; for, besides his many Socialist activities, which never brought him more than eighty pounds a year, he acted as a reporter for the newspaper, the *Sun*, and even sold papers on the side. Young Robert's education was left, therefore, entirely in the hands of his mother. Since Margaret Buchanan was as ardent an Owenite as either her husband or her father, she substituted for religious training a thorough grounding in Owenite socialism. During her son's infancy, both of them took part in two

Owenite communities; and in the Buchanan home the name of
Robert Owen was substituted for that of Jesus Christ.

In 1850 or 1851 the Buchanan family moved to Glasgow, where
the father assumed the editorship of the *Glasgow Sentinel*, a Socialist
newspaper. The boy was entered into a day school in a suburb of
Glasgow near his home. This school was not one of the best, but it
had at least one excellent master who introduced Robert to Latin
and mathematics. After school and on weekends the boy hung
around the *Sentinel* office, where he could listen to the conversation
of leading Socialists and read widely in Socialist literature. But
the move to Glasgow was not a happy one because Buchanan's
father had often lectured there in his missionary days. Severely
Calvinist in its outlook, Glasgow was quick to recall the pugnacious
missionary of ten years earlier and its hatred for him. Nor did young
Robert escape. The citizenry visited the sins of the father upon the
red-haired son by forbidding their sons to play with him or be seen
in his company. With the savage zest of boys in such matters, the
youngsters took up the sport, which was made all the more gratifying by Buchanan's fiery temper. "Don't play with yon laddie, his
father's an infidel!" was their cry to each other.[8]

The effects of such persecution upon a sensitive young lad can
easily be imagined. Buchanan later expressed it:

"It was not . . . until I was taken by my parents to reside in Scotland that
I came face to face with the Dismal Superstition against which my father
and these men, his friends, were passionately struggling. I then learned for
the first time that to fight for human good, to be honest and fearless, to
love the Light, was to be branded as an Enemy of Society and an Atheist.
I saw my father so branded, and I have not forgotten my first horror when
children of my own age avoided me, on the score that I was the son of an
'infidel.' But I learned now that there was more real religion, more holy
zeal for Humanity, in these revolters against the popular creed than in most
of the Christians who preach one faith and practise another.[9]

Three significant effects are apparent in this statement. First, the
taunts of his persecutors completed Buchanan's identification with
his father and the father's Owenite socialism. Second, he was
driven to align himself with his father's rejection of religion and to
regard the forces of orthodoxy as cruel and oppressive. Third,
the mockery of the Glasgow children and their shunning him
because they considered him an infidel left scars upon his consciousness that never healed. He went through life convinced that

he was a religious outcast condemned by the rest of men. It is no mere coincidence that the theme of the outcast, the man accursed, dominates his religious poetry; and in his epic, *The City of Dream*, his religious autobiography, he presents himself as Ishmael, the religious outcast, "whose hand is against every man, and every man's hand against him."[10]

Possibly because of the unpleasantness of the Glasgow environment, Buchanan's parents sent him to another boarding school on the island of Bute. But, when he became homesick, he easily persuaded them to allow him to remain at home to attend day school at the Glasgow Academy. After the academy, he entered the Glasgow High School, studying Latin, French, and English literature. In the literary subjects at least he must have done reasonably well, for he had already made up his mind to follow a literary career. His ambitions were encouraged by his mother and by Hugh Macdonald, an employee of his father, who, besides being a journalist, was something of a poet. Probably with the connivance of Buchanan's father, Macdonald delighted young Robert by buying his first long poem for half a crown. It was published in the *Glasgow Times*, another paper which had come under the control of his father.

After completing high-school requirements, Buchanan entered the University of Glasgow in 1856, taking courses in Latin and Greek. He was assigned to a mild and gentle tutor who saw little of him because Robert had developed a passion for the theater and frequently used his father's position to obtain free passes. The Theatre Royal became his school, and his academic career was neglected. Aside from his interest in the theater, the most important aspect of Buchanan's university career was probably the formation of the first great friendship of his life. This was with David Gray, another ambitious young poet, three years older than Buchanan, and the son of a humble weaver who lived on the outskirts of Glasgow. David had originally intended to enter the ministry of the Free Church of Scotland, but a reading of William Wordsworth's poems at fourteen had filled him with a burning desire to be a poet. The boys' common ambition cemented their friendship. They read and discussed poetry until late at night. In the library of Buchanan's father they delved into the works of Chaucer, Drayton, Milton, and Shakespeare. Their reverence for Wordsworth led them to make at least one journey to the Hebrides, where they visited the Pools of Cladich near Oban and Loch Corruisk on the Isle of Skye, scenes so enchanting to Buchanan that they drew him back in 1866 when he sought to recover his health.

Buchanan's hopes for literary renown were intensified by Gray, whose thirst for poetic fame was an obsession. Gray's error lay in a far greater desire for the fame than for true mastery of and achievement in the art, an error that he at least aided in imparting to Buchanan. To the end of his life, Robert sought the fame and the gold at the end of the literary rainbow, never realizing that he had missed the true road to greatness and was traveling a false, circuitous path that led nowhere. He was always more interested in what was said of his works than in the works themselves; consequently, he usually wrote in a hurry, seldom taking either the time or pains to polish and improve. Had he never met Gray, the impetuous young Robert might conceivably have fallen into the same error; Gray's influence made the pitfall inescapable.

The two tyros early formed the conviction that to reach their goals they must make their mark in the literary capital of Britain— London. But, since literary history afforded many dire examples of what often happened to unknowns in the great city, they sought to establish a beachhead by making contact with some of the city's most noted literary authorities. During 1857 and 1858 they sent a series of ambitious letters to such men as Hepworth Dixon, editor of the *Athenaeum*; George Henry Lewes, critic, journalist, and mentor of George Eliot; Bryan Waller Proctor, Socialist and poet; Sydney Dobell, critic and poet; and Richard Monckton Milnes, biographer of John Keats, politician, and friend of the famous.[11] The letters requested the recipients to read the accompanying samples of the young men's poems and to render a verdict as to whether they might successfully pursue literary careers. Of course, a favorable verdict just might bring a kind offer of aid to place the neophytes on the first rungs of the literary ladder.

Their efforts met with partial success. Lewes replied cautiously to Buchanan that in the samples sent him he had discerned a real faculty, "and perhaps a future poet. I say 'perhaps' because I do not know your age, and because there are so many poetical blossoms which never come to fruit . . . ."[12] Gray received an equally favorable response from Dobell. Although Lewes and Proctor warned earnestly that literature was at best an uncertain venture that one should not undertake without considerable forethought, such words were unheeded; for the two would-be poets were already intoxicated with dreams of success.

Both young men had by this time more than ambition to spur them on. Buchanan's father's mismanagement of his newspapers had brought financial difficulty in 1856. By 1859, he was bankrupt and in court trying to explain his operations. The family was on the verge of poverty; and, though the father with characteristic Owenite sanguinity was making plans to start another paper, young Robert realized it was high time to fend for himself. Gray's home was equally unpleasant because his hard-pressed parents had looked to him for help in rearing and educating the rest of their numerous children. When he abandoned the ministry and announced that he was staking all on his chances of becoming a poet, they could not conceal their disapproval.

The home situations rapidly worsened. Buchanan's mother, despite his pleadings, refused to consent to his going to London. Things were at an impasse when Gray received a letter from Richard Monckton Milnes (later Lord Houghton) in reply to Gray's letter begging Milnes to read his poem "The Luggie" and to advise him about its quality. Milnes's strongly affirmative answer decided him to wait no longer. Gray immediately sought out Buchanan, and Buchanan describes their meeting: "For some little time the London scheme had been in abeyance; but, on the 3rd of May, 1860, David came to me, his lips firmly compressed, his eyes full of fire, saying, 'Bob, I'm off to London.' 'Have you funds?' I asked. 'Enough for one, not enough for two,' was the reply. 'If you can get the money anyhow, we'll go together.' On parting we arranged to meet on the evening of the 5th of May in time to catch the five o'clock train."[13] They did not meet, but they left at the time agreed upon from two different stations and on two separate trains, apparently because of a misunderstanding as to the station at which they were to entrain. Consequently, though each arrived in London on schedule, they did not find each other until two or three weeks later.

III *Gaining a Foothold*

Buchanan's arrival in London in May, 1860, was less than auspicious. During the journey he lost his train ticket, and his baggage was impounded at the station for a week. While he was in such sore straits, some of his father's Socialist friends in London came to his rescue with food, shelter, and small sums of money. He and Gray did not meet until near the end of May, when Gray had already contracted tuberculosis by sleeping one cool night in Hyde Park. Gray had called upon Richard Monckton Milnes, who, failing to persuade him to return to Scotland, charitably assisted him with money and clothing and also obtained for him some copying work from which he earned a pittance.

Gray insisted upon moving in with Buchanan, who by this time was leading a precarious and bohemian existence in a garret room at 66 Stamford Street in the dingy neighborhood of Waterloo Bridge. For the next year and a half, while the tuberculosis ravaged Gray's frail physique, he became increasingly a nuisance to his friends and to Buchanan in particular because he had to witness his sufferings and listen to his complaints. Milnes did all he could to help by getting Gray into hospitals—in which Gray refused to stay; by giving him money; by bringing food in his pockets to Stamford Street; and, finally, by prevailing upon Gray to go to his parents' humble home in Glasgow, where his troubles finally ended in his death in December, 1861, shortly after Milnes had managed to have published his most ambitious poem, "The Luggie." In Gray's grim experience, Buchanan had a chance to observe what could happen to any young man alone in London if he neglected his health and if the odds went against him. The glitter of the metropolis did not necessarily promise fame and fortune; it could be a will-o'-the-wisp that led to the grave.

To the end of his life Buchanan identified himself with Gray as a sort of alter ego. During his last days, Gray wrote letters to his friends, urging them to work for fame for his sake and promising that, if it were possible, he would communicate with them from beyond the grave. Undoubtedly, this was also the tenor of his letters to Buchanan and his conversations with him, for throughout his career Buchanan continued to apostrophize his dead friend fondly and intimately and to view him as a poetic secret sharer.

Nevertheless, Buchanan was not so frightened by Gray's fate that he abandoned his own aspirations and returned to Glasgow. He had good reasons for remaining in London; for, by the time of Gray's death in December, 1861, Buchanan's literary career was prospering. Through Gray, he had made the acquaintance of Milnes and Sydney Dobell, both of whom had considerable influence in London literary circles and used their good offices in the Scotsman's behalf. Dobell, for instance, recommended him to Edmund Yates, editor of the newly established magazine, *Temple Bar*, who thereafter published many of Buchanan's early articles and poems. Through some such influence Buchanan also in his first year in London made the acquaintance of Charles Dickens, who bought several of his poems for publication in *All the Year Round*, the magazine Dickens was then editing. Probably through Dickens also, Buchanan published poetry in *Once a Week* and in *Good Words*.

More prestigious than any of these was Buchanan's connection with the *Athenaeum*, rapidly coming to the fore as the leading English reviewing organ, on which he established himself as a staff reviewer. As he himself whimsically observed, he literally wrote criticism for the *Athenaeum* "by the yard," for he delivered his reviews to publisher John Francis, who measured them with a foot rule and paid him ten-and-sixpence a column.[14] Probably his success with the *Athenaeum* aided materially in securing him a second post as reviewer for the *Eclectic Review*. He also formed an acquaintance with Thomas Love Peacock, Romantic poet and novelist, friend of Shelley, and father-in-law of George Meredith. Because Peacock, then in his seventies, was living at Lower Halliford on the Thames, Buchanan went sometime during the summer of 1862 to live nearby so that he might read to him the poems that he was designing for *Undertones*, his first volume of poetry.

Two other acquaintances enlivened these early days and exerted important influences upon Buchanan's career. One of these was William Black, another Glasgowite who had come to London in quest of literary fortune, and who later became a well-known novelist. Although their friendship was soon ended by a difference of opinion, Black's success was one of the factors which later led Buchanan to try his hand at the novel. The other influential friend was Charles Gibbon, another young literary bohemian who shared Buchanan's room at 66 Stamford Street after the departure of Gray. In 1862 Gibbon and Buchanan collaborated on a melodrama called *The Rathboys*, which ran for some weeks at the Standard Theatre and which marks the beginning of Buchanan's career as a dramatist. Later in 1862 Buchanan tried a second play, *The Witchfinder*; but he did not succeed in getting it produced until 1864 when it had a short run at Sadler's Wells. Discouraged with such results, he wrote no more plays until 1874.

In the meantime, he published in *Temple Bar* in the early months of 1861 poems with such Victorian genre titles as "The Dead," "The Dead Baby," "The Outcasts," and "The Destitute." The introduction of the steam-powered press in 1804 and the cheaper, more rapid production of paper in the first quarter of the nineteenth century led to such a proliferation of magazines that by the early 1860's any intelligent, educated young Briton with a facile pen could find a market for his literary wares. Buchanan had the necessary qualifications, especially the facile pen; and a flood of reviews, poems, essays, and stories poured from him. These soon won him a reputation as a young man of talent and created a greater demand for his work, a demand which Buchanan met by working harder and writing faster.

The total effect upon him of this early journalistic success was not good. In combination with the effects of his Owenite upbringing, his haphazard education, the influence of Gray, and the impatience and impulsiveness of his own nature, it only confirmed him in the careless writing habits which stayed with him for life. What he needed was what any young writer needs—the stern discipline to teach him to study much; to think much before he writes at all; then to revise, to recast, to polish at great length. Buchanan had real genius, as the Victorian critics of the 1860's and 1870's recognized when they bracketed his name with those of Browning, Tennyson, and Arnold. It was unfortunate that the realities of his life and the shortcomings of his character stood in the way of his fullest development.

His early success handicapped him also in that it increased his responsibilities and his burdens. During 1861 his parents moved to London, where his father, inspired by his son's example, hoped to make a living in journalism. However, although Buchanan Senior did manage to secure a few small reportorial assignments on some of the London newspapers, his chief support and that of Mrs. Buchanan came from their son. The parents furnished a small house in a London suburb; and Buchanan and Gibbon, responding to the pleading of Buchanan's mother, relinquished the drafty old garret in Stamford Street to move in with them.

This arrangement ended late in 1861 with Buchanan's marriage to Mary Jay, elder sister of Harriett, Buchanan's later biographer. Nothing is known of Mary's background or of the circumstances of their first meeting and subsequent courtship. She was a beautiful girl in her teens when she married Buchanan; he had just passed his twentieth birthday. Certainly, he was old enough in those days of youthful marriages, but his financial circumstances hardly warranted his undertaking the support of a wife.

The union did not turn out altogether fortunately. The young wife was soon afflicted with internal disorders which later developed into cancer, causing her death in 1881. As far as is known, there were no children, though the number of Buchanan's early poems dealing with the theme of a dead baby suggests that they might have had one child who died infancy. For the rest, Harriett hints guardedly of incompatibility between Buchanan and his wife, while Buchanan himself testifies that his wife displayed little interest in poetry.[15] The marriage brought Buchanan still another responsibility in his wife's much younger sister Harriett, who lived with him until his death in 1901.

IV *Friends and Influences*

In addition to desire for fame, the young Scotsman now had an even more stern pressure of financial necessity to goad him onward. Realizing that he would get ahead much more readily if he had the aid of influential friends, he was not slow to seek the acquaintance and good offices of important literary figures. Buchanan was the sort of person to whom others were never indifferent: they either liked him or detested him, and his reactions to them were usually of a reciprocal character and intensity. Never servile nor sycophantish, he had a dogged independence and a blunt manner of speaking which repelled those who demanded agreement and deference as conditions of friendship; but it recommended him to those who valued honesty and forthrightness. As a young man, he had such egoism that it verged upon conceit; consequently, he was never able to interpret adverse criticism of himself or his works as anything but ill-concealed animosity. All these qualities added up to a man who made many acquaintances but few real friends, and whose considerable number of ill-wishers made his literary career almost as stormy and contentious as his father's had been in the service of Owenism.

Buchanan, however, had the prudence to keep his conceit hidden in 1862, when he was casting about for literary connections to further his career. One of his first attempts was in the direction of George H. Lewes as a follow-up to the encouraging letter Lewes had written him in Glasgow. Lewes had tempered his praise by earnestly advising the young poet to continue writing and refining his verse, but by no means to seek to publish it until he had matured and mastered his craft. Now Buchanan wrote Lewes that he had faithfully followed his advice and that, after two years in London, he felt ready to embark upon his poetic career.

There came an invitation from Lewes; and Buchanan soon presented himself at the Priory, North Bank, Regent's Park, where Lewes was living with his common-law wife, Mary Ann Evans, who, under the pseudonym George Eliot, was already famous as the authoress of *Adam Bede* and *Silas Marner*, and whose *Romola* was about to be serialized in the *Cornhill* magazine. Buchanan was favorably impressed with Lewes, whom he described as "a little, bright, not ill-looking man of between forty and fifty, with a magnificent forehead, bright, intelligent eyes, and a manner full of intellectual grace. True, he was not physically beautiful. The great defects of the face were the coarse, almost sensual-looking mouth, with its protruding teeth, partly covered by a bristly moustache, and the small, retreating chin; but when the face lighted up and the eyes sparkled and the mouth began its eloquent discourse, every imperfection was forgotten."[16] As for Lewe's cohabitant, George Eliot, he felt only antipathy, which she probably repaid in full.

Through Lewes and his consort, Buchanan came into contact with the Positivism of Auguste Comte, which created intense interest in English intellectual circles in the 1860's and 1870's. J. S. Mill wrote upon it at length, as did Lewes himself; for both he and George Eliot were confirmed Positivists. Buchanan was strongly drawn to the new philosophy because of its agreement with the teachings of Owen, its attacks upon religion, and its tenet of the perfectibility of man through his own efforts. Buchanan was, however, reluctant to accept unreservedly the doctrine of Positivism because he disliked its materialism and its vagueness about the hereafter. He worried about the matter at great length, threshed it out pro and con throughout his poetry, and finally toward the close of his life settled upon a composite of some elements of Positivism, some of Christianity, and some of his own distillation.

His dislike for George Eliot did not prevent Buchanan from calling frequently at the Lewes and Eliot home at the Priory, a favorite gathering place for Victorian literary celebrities. There he met in 1864 Robert Browning, whom he revered above all other living poets. The circumstances of the meeting were not unlike those under which Boswell met Samuel Johnson. When Buchanan begged the "Sibyl," as he called George Eliot, to introduce him to the great poet, she obliged by inviting him to a gathering at the Priory at which Browning was to be present, and she performed the introduction herself. Buchanan was disappointed; he had expected to find an earth-shaker, one who would speak as from Mount Sinai and leave him awed and trembling; but he found instead a quiet, courteous Victorian gentleman who took him aside into a corner of the room and listened sympathetically to Buchanan's story of David Gray, who had once dreamed of going to Florence, of throwing himself upon Browning's generosity, and of curing his tuberculosis by staying with Browning in the beneficent Italian climate.

He and Browning soon became good friends, but their friendship did not run smoothly. They engaged in frequent disputes, which Buchanan usually lost because of the older man's ready vocabulary; their relationship was that of teacher and pupil rather than of equals. On one occasion when Buchanan spoke in praise of Whitman, Browning flared up in denunciation of the American bard because of the immorality of his verse—a view Buchanan ascribed to jealousy since he did not credit Browning with having read any of Whitman's poems. The consequence of their differences was that their friendship cooled. By 1888 all cordiality between them had vanished. Buchanan remarked with some bitterness that at the Royal Academy dinner of that year Browning treated him with marked coldness and sneered at him to a mutual acquaintance as a mere writer of plays. Fortunately, other friendships turned out more happily. Together with other bohemians of literature and the drama, Buchanan became a regular caller on Sundays at the home of the minor playwright Westland Marston. Here he made the acquaintance of Herman Vezin and W. G. Willis, dramatists, and of Dinah Mulock Craik, authoress of the popular novel *John Halifax Gentleman*. Graciously, she invited the young climber to her home and gave him the free run of her library. In 1865, while summering with his wife and sister-in-law at Bexhill, then a little village on the south coast of England, Buchanan also became firm friends with Roden Noel, the poet son of the Earl of Gainsborough. Despite Buchanan's Socialist prejudices and his religious skepticism, he and Noel developed an abiding affection for each other which continued until Noel's death in 1894. Noel, who had been designed for the church, possessed a devout faith that contrasted with Buchanan's fretful questioning of all creeds; but these differences did not stand in the way of their mutual regard.

During 1884 Buchanan made his only visit to the United States. While in Philadelphia in connection with the production of his play *Alone in London*, he made the short journey to Camden, New Jersey, to greet Walt Whitman, whom he had consistently hailed since his early days in London as one of the greatest poets of the age and whom he had aided more substantially in 1876 with his letters to the press urging British financial contributions to the American poet. Unlike Browning, Whitman fulfilled Buchanan's image of him. The two men talked about various matters: in exchange for news of the British poets, especially Tennyson, Whitman told of the American literary scene. Buchanan's sympathies were aroused, and a feeling of kinship was established when he learned how Whitman had been ostracized by Bostonians such as James Russell Lowell and Oliver Wendell Holmes. The two found another common bond in their love of humanity in the mass and in their conviction of the intrinsic worth of even the lowest mortal.

Buchanan was deeply impressed with the apparent poverty and simplicity of Whitman's mode of life. Whitman showed him over his small house: his bedroom, his armchair, his trunks of books and papers. Buchanan came away convinced that he had been in the company of a great poet and a great martyr. Extravagantly, he acclaimed Whitman as greater than Socrates and as even a modern approximation of Christ. His belief in the Sage of Camden never wavered. In 1887, he published a short essay in which he urged his readers to send financial aid to Whitman; and, in 1898, he included in his *New Rome* the poems "Socrates in Camden" and "Walt Whitman" as his tender memorial on the occasion of the American's death.

V *The Slings and Arrows*

As we have indicated, a man of Buchanan's combative and egotistic temperament was bound to make enemies. Born and reared in the spirit of controversy, he went through life with a chip-on-the-shoulder attitude which earned him a wide circle of ill-wishers and kept him embroiled in a succession of futile quarrels (discussed in Chapter 2) to the detriment of his literary career and his peace of mind. Buchanan's tribulations did not all come from his quarrels with others, although many of them did spring from the same basic shortcomings in his character. Early in his career, at the very time when the mounting demands upon him should have impressed him with the necessity of husbanding his finances, he displayed a marked inability to handle money. After the death of his father in 1866, illness and financial straits forced him to move himself and his three women—his wife, his mother, and Harriett Jay—to Oban in the Scottish Highlands until 1873. From there they moved to Rossport, Ireland, for three more years, apparently because it was even cheaper to live there than at Oban.

In Ireland, Buchanan's situation improved. He had obviously concluded that poetry and magazine articles alone would not earn him a comfortable living, for in 1874 he began to cast about for more lucrative work. In March of that year, after a ten-year hiatus, he returned to the theater with the play *The Madcap Prince*, which brought him a fair return; and in 1876 he published his first novel, *The Shadow of the Sword*, as a serial in the *Gentleman's Magazine* for a hundred and eighty guineas. After the serialization was completed, the novel in book form achieved considerable success. In June, 1876, his play *Corinne* at the Lyceum in London was an artistic failure but a financial success because Buchanan, wise in the ways of theater managers, had insisted on being paid in advance.

From 1876 Buchanan devoted more and more attention to his novels and plays. In the 1880's and 1890's it was not unusual for him to produce as many as two novels and three or four plays a year, together with several critical essays in magazines and a volume of poetry. He made considerable money; if he had used it wisely, his financial worries would have been over; but, as Harriett Jay says, he was always in arrears because he persisted in living beyond his income.[17] The inevitable resulted on August 24, 1894, when his extravagance and generosity, together with a disastrous speculation in the production of his play *A Social Butterfly*, brought him to a court of bankruptcy, as his father had been in Glasgow nearly forty years earlier. When Buchanan suffered a stroke in 1900 and lay for almost eight months a helpless invalid, only the charity of his friends saved him the humiliation of becoming a public charge.

Quite naturally, the effect of his prodigality upon his literary work was harmful. To earn more and more money, he was forced to write with ever greater haste and less care. Although here and there he took considerable pains with a few works which lay close to his heart, many of the productions of his late years show a distinct lessening of quality. But, if haste and waste frustrated his literary talents, so did his continuing, almost constant, fretting over religion.

Buchanan could readily accept the Owenite dogma that political despots had used organized religion to keep humanity in intellectual and political bondage, a dogma that was reinforced by his acceptance of Positivism; but he could not rid himself of the gnawing suspicion that the larger claims of religion might have an essential truth that the Owenites had missed.

Buchanan could warmly espouse Owen's teaching of the necessity and practicability of social, governmental, and economic justice for all men—beliefs which were also seconded by Positivism and by the growing Victorian enthusiasm for the democratic principle—but he could not agree that the attainment of such goals would bring universal happiness. Familiar with the disillusionment that followed the passage of the Reform Bills of 1832, 1867, and 1884, he remained skeptical of the advantages of adding mere numbers to the electorate. Nor was he so enchanted with the uses of machinery and science as his father and Robert Owen had been. He had lived longer than they with the Industrial Revolution and had come to regard the new "miracles" as only commonplaces, as not really affecting the fundamentals of life.

Buchanan's mind, therefore, had to probe beyond the mere surface of material things in a desperate endeavor to discover the presence of a loving God and an assurance of a personal immortality for himself and his loved ones. His strong strain of Celtic mysticism and his passionate yearnings prompted him to believe that there must be such a presence and such an immortality. On the other hand, his stubborn Scottish realism, reinforced by his father's scoffings and by the Victorian agnostic's demand for a visible sign of the deity's existence, led him to insist upon tangible evidence as a precondition to belief.

He was thus an unhappy man, a man pulled both ways by forces he could neither resist nor resolve. Throughout his life he remained on religious dead center, unable wholly to reject or to believe. Unlike Matthew Arnold, who could view his religious doubts with a classical calm, or Alfred Lord Tennyson, whose questing ended in faith, Buchanan was tormented by his inner conflict. The effect was harmful to him as a person and as a literary artist. His brooding upon his problem magnified it so much that it beclouded his entire horizon and robbed him of that clarity of vision so essential to the artist if he is to attain the ultimate of his capabilities. His most ambitious works, like *The City of Dream* and *The Wandering Jew*, show only too clearly that the city was filled with nightmarish shapes and shadows and that the real Wandering Jew was the tortured theological vagrant, Robert Buchanan.

Understandably, Buchanan's times of greatest crisis followed closely upon the deaths of his loved ones. The first of these came in 1866 with the death of his father—an event that transformed what had been a philosophical question discussed over tea with Lewes and George Eliot at the Priory into a terrible reality before which he recoiled. The father whom he loved and who symbolized atheism had slipped into the unknown. If Calvinistic Christianity was right, then his father was certainly damned; if it was wrong, Buchanan Senior had only met the common fate and had vanished into nothingness. Buchanan's resolution of the question is indicated in *The Wandering Jew*—begun soon after his father's death but not published until 1893—in which he found Christ and Christianity to be fraudulent. Significantly, he dedicated the poem to his father's memory.

Before Buchanan's own death on June 10, 1901, he had to undergo the agony of two more bereavements: that of his wife after a long and painful illness of cancer on November, 1881, and of his mother, the lodestar of his life, in November, 1894. Both these events plunged him once more into all the old agonized questioning and searching about religion. The death of his mother was especially painful and depressing, and his entry in his diary after her funeral is heavy with the spiritual gloom that closed around him:

... why have I not the courage to admit ... that Death is the inevitable end of all consciousness, and the dream of another life is simply a mirage certain to fade away? Cardinal Newman himself admitted with a sigh that Nature as we know it gave no indication whatever of divine goodness or beneficence, and that to believe in God at all, blind faith was necessary. I have no such faith; but I retain my hope, simply and solely because without it life is unexplainable. If this is the only life we are to know, there is certainly no God, and if there is no God, life is certainly, as I have said, a mere drunkard's dream[18]

Here, in his own words, was his dilemma. He could not accept the despairing view of James Thomson's "The City of Dreadful Night," that life was a meaningless experience without reason or design, without hope of immortality. Nor was he able to share the strong faith of Tennyson's "In Memoriam." Pulled in opposite directions by the forces of belief and unbelief, Buchanan lived on a spiritual rack through most of his life and went to his grave with the problem unsolved.

CHAPTER 2

The Man of Controversy

BUCHANAN'S role as critic and castigator of his times made certain that his career would be stormy. Not only were his views in opposition to the prevailing thought of his day, but his vehemence in argument lacerated sensibilities and created enemies. He was especially fierce with those whose actions violated his Owenite principles or his Victorian idealism. As a result, he attacked Swinburne for outraging Victorian canons of decency, ridiculed Dante Gabriel Rossetti for the lustful tone of many of his poems and for his lack of sympathy for a prostitute, took exception to George Eliot for her mechanistic view of life and character, and assailed yellow journalism for its underhanded attacks upon defenseless people, especially women.

He also castigated Thomas Carlyle for championing such ruthless individuals as Frederick the Great of Prussia and for being unconcerned for the common man and his problems. He denounced Rudyard Kipling for trumpeting the glory of war and of British imperialism. He preached against the menace of State Socialism and its oppression of the individual. He attacked Thomas Henry Huxley for his disparaging remarks about the Salvation Army. He urged the abolishment of rigid censorship. He strongly opposed the rise of Naturalism in literature. He dared to oppose Gladstone on the sanctity of marriage, and he argued for divorce as the right of the individual in the case of an unhappy marriage.

Undoubtedly, Buchanan's literary strife was highly injurious to his career. Not only did his polemics take a great deal of his time; they also created enemies who hurt him in literary circles. His many attacks and disputes fostered in the public mind an image that his enemies had labored to create—of a carping, caviling fellow who would assail anybody for any reason whatsoever. This image was not an accurate one, for Buchanan fought only for principles close to his heart. They were his real, his only, religion; and he stood ready to sacrifice all for them. His family motto, he said, was "Tell the truth and shame the Devil!"[1] To this motto he remained true, no matter what the cost. As time went on, therefore, his popularity lessened—and so did his income. This price he paid willingly and intentionally, if not gladly.

I *The Fleshly Controversy*

Buchanan's longest and most involved altercation was the Fleshly Controversy in which he became embroiled with a host of opponents, but his chief foes were Algernon Charles Swinburne, William Michael Rossetti, and Dante Gabriel Rossetti. His initial quarrel was with Swinburne, but William Michael gratuitously meddled in the dispute to give aid to the sorely beset Swinburne and brought down upon himself and his brother the full force of Buchanan's wrath. Ironically, it was Dante Rossetti, who had done nothing to anger Buchanan and whom Buchanan confessed later he had never even met, who became the chief target of the Scotsman's blows. Such a focus was unfortunate for Buchanan also; for Dante Rossetti had a wide circle of friends, disciples, and acquaintances, many of whom rallied to his support. Buchanan, except for three or four daring souls who came out in print in his behalf in the early days of the controversy, fought alone. He fought valiantly, though not always wisely and skillfully, and the sheer weight of numbers bore him down. With some justice Buchanan could say in later years that, had he not been made of sturdy fiber, he might have suffered a fate like that of Dante Rossetti.[2]

Nowhere have I discovered any mention of a personal meeting of Buchanan and Swinburne, but I believe such a meeting took place, that it was an unfortunate encounter, and that it was the original incitement to the Fleshly Controversy. There were many possibilities of such a meeting since both young men were friends and protégés of Richard Monckton Milnes, later Lord Houghton, who had a sinister penchant for bringing opposite personalities together at breakfast in his London home, introducing subjects on which he knew them to disagree, and then watching the sparks fly. It seems unlikely that he would have missed matching two such natural antagonists as Buchanan and Swinburne. But, if Milnes did restrain himself, the literary orbits of Buchanan and Swinburne touched at so many other points that their meeting is highly probable. Coming to London in the early 1860's to pursue literary careers, both wrote for several of the same organs, including the *Athenaeum* and the *Spectator*; both published with Moxon; both were acquaint-

ed with George Henry Lewes and George Eliot and visited their
home at the Priory. Both also knew Tennyson and Browning;
both were friends of the playwright Westland Marston; and both
frequented the Reading Room of the British Museum and used it
for study and research.

If they did meet, they could hardly have failed to strike fire from
each other because they were natural antagonists. Vain, outspoken,
and strongly opinionated, both lacked tact and paid little heed to
the social graces of tolerance and courtesy. Swinburne, whose
ancestral home was in Northumberland, a few miles from the border,
despised the Scotch; and Scotsman Buchanan had as little use for
the English aristocracy. Swinburne, Etonian and Oxonian, was the
product of nobility and affluence; Buchanan was a man of the
people. Swinburne paid lip service to the republican ideal but showed
no concern for the masses of poor and underprivileged. Buchanan
was indifferent to political revolution but was strongly devoted to the
down-and-outers who thronged the London streets. Swinburne
was loud in his praise of the estheticism of Charles Baudelaire
and the Pre-Raphaelitism of Dante Gabriel Rossetti; Buchanan's
sturdy Scottish spirit scorned such cults as foreign ideologies,
as false and effeminate.

Whatever may or may not have taken place behind the scenes, the
first overt instance of trouble between the two came early in 1866
when Bertram Payne, editor of Moxon's Publishing Company,
took away from Buchanan an edition of the poems of John Keats
that had been assigned him and gave it to Swinburne. Swinburne's
fierce joy in this opportunity "of trampling on a Scotch Poetaster,"
as he wrote to William Michael Rossetti, is a possible indication
that he had personal knowledge of Buchanan and did not like
him.[3] Whether Buchanan blamed Swinburne for Payne's high-
handed deed, we do not know; certainly, he would view his successful rival with some rancor.

The second act of the drama began in late July, 1866, when Swinburne published his affront to Victorian morality and decency,
his *Poems and Ballads*. In such poems as "Anactoria," "Hermaph-
roditus," "Phaedra," "Dolores," "Faustine," "Fragoletta," and
"Laus Veneris," to mention only a few, Swinburne gave free reign
to the aberrative tendencies of his nature. The result was a bomb-
shell to Victorian England. A host of reviewers leaped to the ramparts
to repel this Gothic invader of the temple of morality, and Buchanan

was one of the first and fiercest. In his review, which appeared in
the *Athenaeum* on August 4, 1866,[4] his tone and manner are those
of a Victorian schoolmaster taking a nasty boy to the woodshed
in punishment for an intolerable offense against the proprieties.
Swinburne's chief fault, Buchanan avers, is that he is "deliberately
and impertinently insincere as an artist . . . and is unclean for the
mere sake of uncleanness,—" and is, therefore, "either no poet at
all, or a poet degraded from his high estate and utterly and miserably
lost to the Muses." He is "Gito, seated in the tub of Diogenes,
conscious of the filth and whining at the stars." Buchanan closes
by speculating that the young poet may have been led toward ruin
by "evil advisers," and he counsels him to turn away from them
before it is too late, or "his very parasites will abandon him, and the
purer light, pouring in his sick eyes, will agonize and perhaps end
him."

This review contains a variety of implications. The worst is the
allusion to Gito, a character in the *Satyricon* of Gaius Petronius,
Master of the Revels at the court of Nero, which has connotations of
pederasty and homosexuality. Gossip of this sort about Swinburne,
thanks to his antics and loose talk, had made its way about London
literary circles. But the reference to the evil advisers and the earnest
tone of Buchanan's advice to depart from them suggest that he had
specific knowledge of Swinburne's relationship with Dante Gabriel
Rossetti, whose disciple Swinburne had been since 1857, and with
William Michael Rossetti, with whom he had been closely associated. Significantly, Buchanan's view of Swinburne as a rash
young fellow in the hands of evil advisers was precisely that of
most of the older people in the poet's life, including his parents,
Lady Trevelyan, John Ruskin, Alfred Tennyson, Robert Browning,
and probably Richard Monckton Milnes, who, ironically, was not
above reproach himself in his encouragement of Swinburne's
abnormal tendencies. It is highly probable that most of Buchanan's
information about Swinburne's private life and associates came from
Milnes. It is not unlikely that Buchanan may have heard Milnes,
Tennyson, or Browning discussing the ominous aspects of Swinburne's career and wishing that something could be done to save
him from disaster. The internal evidence in Buchanan's review
indicates that his intent was at least in part to point out to a young
fellow poet the error of his ways. Most of the other leading Victorian
reviewers seconded Buchanan's judgment of *Poems and Ballads*.

The result was humiliating in the extreme for Swinburne. Payne of Moxon's immediately withdrew the book from publication. Swinburne settled with John Camden Hotten, a minor publisher with an unsavory reputation of publishing pornography, to bring it out. Before he could do so, Buchanan took another fling at the hapless poet in a mocking poem, "The Session of the Poets," in the *Spectator* in September, 1866. Apparently based upon one of Swinburne's escapades at Moxon's gathering for its authors on or about December 13, 1865, an event at which Swinburne drank too much, insulted Tennyson, and made a general nuisance of himself, the poem describes the climax of the evening thus:

> *Up jumped, with his neck stretching out like a gander*
> *Master Swinburne, and squeal'd, glaring out thro' his hair,*
> *"All Virtue is bosh! Hallelujah for Landor!*
> *I disbelieve wholly in everything! There!"*
>
> *With language so awful he dared then to treat 'em,—*
> *Miss Ingelow fainted in Tennyson's arms,*
> *Poor Arnold rush'd out, crying "Soecl' inficetum!"*
> *And great bards and small bards were full of alarms;*
>
> *Till Tennyson, flaming and red as a gipsy,*
> *Struck his fist on the table and utter'd a shout:*
> *"To the door with the boy! Call a cab! He is tipsy!"*
> *And they carried the naughty young gentleman out.*[5]

Buchanan signed the poem with the pseudonym "Caliban," taken possibly from Browning's "Caliban upon Setebos," published only two years earlier in 1864. Further to conceal his tracks, he injected himself into the gathering with this unflattering allusion:

> *There sat, looking moony, conceited, and narrow,*
> *Buchanan,—who, finding, when foolish and young,*
> *Apollo asleep on a coster-girl's barrow,*
> *Straight dragged him away to see somebody hung.*

The poem consorts well with the *Athenaeum* review. It portrays Swinburne as a naughty, effeminate boy trying to attract attention to himself by denying existing standards of morality and virtue and by using forbidden language and allusions in a mixed gathering. It could not fail to ruffle his feathers by giving wide publicity to a disgraceful incident that Swinburne would rather have forgotten, and it carried the suggestion that, if he persisted in such conduct, he would have to be ostracized from decent society—an admonition quite similar to that with which Buchanan had concluded the review.

Swinburne's letters to Joseph Knight, George Powell, and William Rossetti show that both the review and the poem caused him considerable personal disturbance and chagrin.[6] William Rossetti testifies that Caliban was soon identified as Buchanan.[7] In November, 1866, when Swinburne published his *Notes on Poems and Reviews*, asserting that nothing in *Poems and Ballads* should be taken as an expression of his own views or beliefs, he added a sneer at Buchanan's poems "Liz" and "Nell" with the veiled allusion that "If the Muse of the minute will not feast with 'gig-men' and their wives, she must mourn with costermongers and their trulls."[8] In Swinburne's later *Under the Microscope*, he admitted that Buchanan was his target.[9]

A far more grievous cut was aimed at the Scotsman in William Rossetti's small book, *Swinburne's Poems and Ballads*, published a week or two after Swinburne's *Notes*, and with the same purpose of defending Swinburne from the expected onslaughts of inimical reviewers when *Poems and Ballads* came into their hands. The very first sentence of William's book offered the insult: "The advent of a new great poet is sure to cause a commotion of one kind or another; and it would be hard were this otherwise in times like ours, when the advent of even so poor and pretentious a poetaster as a Robert Buchanan stirs storms in teapots."[10] This direct, ill-natured assault upon a man who had apparently done little or nothing to him personally was not in keeping with the calm and judicious tone that William strove to maintain in his writings. Nor was it his custom to make the quarrels of others outside his own family his own. The only explanation of this burst of anger that comes readily to mind is that he had interpreted the "evil advisers" of Buchanan's review of *Poems and Ballads* as aimed at him and his brother and was seeking to hit back.

Buchanan had never before been so savagely attacked in print. The probability is that he well understood what had called forth the insult and realized that in William Rossetti he was dealing with a fierce, mature adversary who would grant no quarter. In Buchanan's later writings in the Fleshly Controversy he continued to regard Swinburne as a wayward boy; but, when he dealt with anybody named Rossetti, his tone was stern and grim. In this instance, he contented himself with a rather mild review of *Notes on Poems and Reviews* in the *Athenaeum* of November 3, 1866.[11] Buchanan, though he yielded not an inch in his condemnation of *Poems and Ballads*, praised his adversary's *Atalanta in Calydon* and reiterated his hope that Swinburne would yet mend his ways and win the laurels that were within the reach of his genius. It is ominously significant that he made no mention at all of William Rossetti's book and the insult offered therein.

Swinburne permitted himself one more veiled rejoinder to Buchanan in his lengthy article "Mr. Arnold's New Poems" in the *Fortnightly Review* in October, 1867. Taking exception to Wordsworth's theory that the true poetic "vision" and "divine faculty" of inspiration automatically insure technical excellence in the verse of even an untutored poet, Swinburne exclaims:

> Such talk as this of Wordsworth's is the poison of poor souls like David Gray. Men listen, and depart with the belief that they have this faculty or this vision which alone, they are told, makes the poet; and once imbued with that belief, soon pass or slide from the inarticulate to the articulate stage of debility and disease. Inspiration foiled and impotent is a piteous thing enough, but friends and teachers of this sort make it ridiculous as well. A man can no more win a place among poets by dreaming of it or lusting after it than he can win by dream or desire a woman's beauty or a king's command.[12]

When Swinburne published this essay in his *Essays and Studies* of 1875, he added a long footnote attacking the dead Gray with the utmost scorn.[13] Buchanan later cited this reference as the provocation for his attack upon Dante Gabriel Rossetti in 1871. But Buchanan's memory deceived him, for no such note occurred in the original article. Nevertheless, what was in the article was sufficient to roil his temper, for he cherished Gray's memory and rightly interpreted Swinburne's patronizing tone as a deliberate insult. Likewise, the poetic philosophy that Swinburne ascribed to Gray was also Buchanan's, and the shoe pinched.

The publication of William Rossetti's edition of Shelley in 1870 gave Buchanan an opportunity to settle partially his score with that gentleman. Again he did so with an *Athenaeum* review in which he found William deficient in the knowledge, the critical insight, and the good taste requisite for such an important editorial task. But with more moderation than William had shown him, Buchanan closed by conceding that William had done some service by pointing out a number of errors in the existing text of the poems.[14] Undoubtedly, William could hardly have been pleased with this largely negative view of his most ambitious literary undertaking to date. Just as certainly he must have recognized that Buchanan had paid him back in his own coin—finding him as incapable as a critic as he had Buchanan as a poet.

Such was the state of affairs when Dante Gabriel Rossetti published his *Poems* in the latter part of April, 1870. In a precarious condition of mind and body from repeated overdoses of laudanum and alcohol, together with the harmful effects of the bohemian life he had been leading for years, he allowed himself to be persuaded to exhume the manuscript of the verses which, in an act of self-imposed penance, he had buried in his wife's coffin in 1862. He added to the manuscript many poems he had written in the intervening years, a good many of which, as Oswald Doughty shows in his biography of Rossetti, grew out of his illicit passion for Mrs. Jane Morris. With Swinburne's assistance, Rossetti brought the volume to birth and then awaited eagerly the critical results of his venture.

Publication had necessitated the overcoming of a mental obstacle: Rossetti was ridden with an abnormal fear of public censure, a fear so great that he had for years shunned public exhibitions of his pictures and had resisted the urgings of his friends to publish his poems. True, he had printed a few of them in magazines from time to time; but, until 1870, he had refused to bring them out in book form and expose himself to the scrutiny of the reviewers. His reluctance was intensified by the knowledge that several of his poems violated Victorian standards of decency. He was well aware of the details of Swinburne's catastrophe only four years before and of the part played by the ogre Buchanan, for in such an image was Buchanan apparently portrayed to him by Swinburne and William, who also seem to have warned him that he might expect an attack from the Scotsman.

To offset such an attack and to insure a favorable acceptance for his *Poems*, Dante Gabriel Rossetti placed key men at many of the important organs of critical opinion: Swinburne wrote the review for the *Fortnightly*; William Morris, for the *Academy*; Sidney Colvin, for the *Westminster Review, Pall Mall Gazette*, and the *Quarterly*; and Thomas Hake, for the *New Monthly*, and so on. Had Dante Gabriel been contented with a few restrained but laudatory reviews in the leading magazines and papers, all might have been well; and the ruse might have worked successfully.

But there was no restraining such zealots as Swinburne, whose
review in the *Fortnightly* in May, 1870, compared Rossetti with
Shakespeare and proclaimed him the equal, if not the superior, of
Tennyson, Arnold, and Browning. Literary London soon smelled
the odor of puffery, and a few dissonant notes became audible.
Blackwood's Magazine in August, 1870, took Rossetti to task for
the "factitious" character of his poetic reputation, found fault with
the "fleshly imagination" exhibited in "The Blessed Damozel,"
and concluded that his book offered nothing of true poetic value.[15]

Even more negative, as well as more perceptive and more ably
written, was James Russell Lowell's review in the *North American
Review* in October, 1870.[16] It was more an article than a review
because it ran to about forty-three hundred words, and its purview
included the whole matter of Pre-Raphaelitism as well as the
technique and substance of Pre-Raphaelite poetry. Lowell took
quick, disapproving side-glances at the work of Swinburne, William
Morris, and William Rossetti; gave a measure of praise to the verse
of Thomas Woolner and Christina Rossetti; then focused his
attention and trained his critical guns upon Dante Rossetti and
his *Poems*. His article is great criticism in vigorous, sinewy prose;
and it must be numbered among the noted reviews of literary
history. Remarking that most of the encomiums had come from
Swinburne, Morris, and William Rossetti, he observed that they
were neither competent nor impartial judges of poetic merit and
would, therefore, hardly be taken seriously by those outside the
"cultus" of Pre-Raphaelitism.

As for Pre-Raphaelitism itself, Lowell found all its art, both
poetic and pictorial, at fault because of its "over-strenuousness,"
undirected enthusiasm, and affectation. These same faults, along
with others, are the besetting sins of Dante Rossetti's verse; but he
does give some evidence of taste, technical skill, subtlety, "and a
sort of pictorial sensuousness of conception which gives warmth and
vividness to the imagery that embodies his feelings and desires."
However, says Lowell, Rossetti is too sensual, too absorbed in
himself as a sad, morbid lover, and too erotic to be either exhilarating
or convincing. This morbid sexuality is quite evident in his poem
"Jenny," which blurs "the distinction between morality and immorality" and which might, therefore, be dangerous for some
readers. With Rossetti love tends toward sensual and sexual
appetite, never toward genuine, unselfish devotion.

Unrealistic and unconvincing too is Rossetti's portrayal of medieval life, and Lowell views with strong suspicion any poet, thinker, or artist "who can content himself with his fancies of the thoughts and feelings and views of times past, and who can better please himself with what after all must be more or less unreal phantasmagoria, than with the breathing life around him." Lowell's final judgment is that Rossetti is not a "true poet of any weight, and he thinks it likely "that the fashion of his poetry will very soon pass away and be gone for good" because he is a "writer so affected, sentimental, and painfully self-conscious that the best that can be done in his case is to hope that this book of his, as it has 'unpacked his bosom' of so much that is unhealthy, may have done him more good than it has given others pleasure."

Dante Rossetti's *Poems* is listed in the *Publisher's Circular* for the latter half of April, 1870. Lowell's article appeared in October, 1870, six months later. Buchanan's fateful article, "The Fleshly School of Poetry: Mr. D. G. Rossetti," was published in the *Contemporary Review* for October, 1871, exactly one year after Lowell's and a year and a half after Rossetti's book. Not only was Buchanan's criticism too late to be styled a review, but its length of approximately seventy-five hundred words, nearly twice that of Lowell's, clearly establishes it as an article. A collation of the two pieces makes it quite clear that Buchanan patterned his article after Lowell's in tone, form, and substance, though with sufficient dissimilarity in content and emphasis to show freedom of viewpoint and expression and to shield him from a charge of plagiarism. It is clear from Buchanan's extensive quotations that he had Lowell's article before him as he wrote, as well as Swinburne's and Morris's reviews of the *Poems*.

Like Lowell, Buchanan condemns the entire Pre-Raphaelite cult as affected and insincere. It is, he exclaims, "merely one of many sub-Tennysonian schools expanded to supernatural dimensions, and endeavouring by affectations all its own to over-shadow its connection with the great original."[17] Like Lowell, also, he finds the Pre-Raphaelites guilty of praising each other's writings far beyond their true merits. They have, he sneers, formed a veritable "Mutual Admiration School" for this purpose and have so far succeeded in befooling the British public. In their poetry he finds that Swinburne and Morris show occasional flashes of real talent, but Dante Rossetti is clearly inferior to both, though he is not so "glibly imitative" as Morris nor so "transcendently superficial" as Swinburne.[18]

Turning attention to William Rossetti, to whom *Poems* is dedicated, Buchanan exclaims that he "will perhaps be known to bibliographers as the editor of the worst edition of Shelley which has yet seen the light."[19] Thus does he even his old score for William's calling him a poetaster; and thus deftly, though somewhat deviously, does he follow Lowell's lead of stultifying three of Dante Rossetti's leading encomiasts. Further to clinch the matter, Buchanan quotes satirically from Swinburne's and Morris's reviews, laying especial emphasis upon some of Swinburne's more extravagant phrases like "golden affluence," "jewel-coloured words," and "consummate fleshly sculpture." Throughout the remainder of his article Buchanan's procedure is to quote passages from the *Poems* and then fling these phrases at Rossetti like stones.

Since Buchanan's chief indictment of Dante Gabriel is on the score of sexuality and sensuality, again following Lowell's lead, Buchanan picks up "fleshly" and makes it and its cognate forms the keynote of his article and his title. Both Buchanan and Lowell find that such sensuality is one of the hallmarks of Pre-Raphaelitism, as also is the affected and insincere medievalism so prevalent in both the poetry and painting of the group. In Rossetti's case, both Lowell and Buchanan condemn Dante Gabriel's description of the passion of love as without conscience or feeling; and both use the word *morbid* to characterize it. Both single out "Jenny" as an exemplification of this fault. Both point to his "A Stream's Secret" and "The Last Confession" as among his best love poems, but both insist that even in these is the taint of sensuality.

Other similarities are both numerous and evident. Both Lowell and Buchanan look askance at Dante Gabriel's shying away from publishing his poems in book form for a long period. Both pay particular attention to the pictorial quality of his verse. Both praise "The Blessed Damozel" as his best poem, and both admit the excellence of his translation of Dante's *Vita Nuova*. The *Germ*, the early journal of the Pre-Raphaelites, comes in for derisive mention by both men. Both accuse Dante Gabriel of closely imitating Browning in some of the more dramatic poems, such as "Jenny"; but Buchanan goes a step further to insist that the tone of *Poems* has been taken from Tennyson and that the style and technique of the sonnets have been inspired by Mrs. Browning. Both complain that his only care is for the form of his verse, that he is deficient in thought and imagination.

Both find Rossetti guilty in the love poems of being completely absorbed in his own reactions and emotions to the exclusion of any concern for the woman in the case. Both are fearful that the fleshly poets may infect and harm others, especially those unaware of the basic immorality so subtly inculcated. Both hold the opinion that the fleshly poets will pass and be forgotten because there is little real merit in them. Both render a final judgment that Dante Gabriel is a clever charlatan but not a true poet, and Buchanan concludes by quoting Lowell's key judicial sentence and says it expresses his opinion also, adding that, if Dante Gabriel were younger, there might be hope that he would overcome his faults, but "his 'maturity' is fatal."[20]

Not only is Buchanan's article considerably longer than Lowell's: it differs in some significant respects. First, Buchanan injects himself into the article as he had into the "Session of the Poets," and doubtless for the same reason of trying to conceal his identity. He begins by imagining that the contemporary English poets are cast in the various roles of Shakespeare's *Hamlet*, with Tennyson and Browning alternating as Hamlet; Arnold, as Horatio; Buchanan, as Cornelius; Swinburne and Morris, as Rosencrantz and Guildenstern; and Dante Rossetti, as Osric. Later, Buchanan states that Rossetti's "Jenny" shows signs of having been suggested by "Mr. Buchanan's quasi-lyrical poems," especially his "Artist and Model."[21] He exclaims in wonder at Rossetti's having so far escaped censure for his poems, which are much more offensive than Swinburne's *Poems and Ballads*. Swinburne, however, was only a naughty boy, but Rossetti is a mature man and should be held much more responsible.

Rossetti's most offensive, most fleshly poem is "Nuptial Sleep" because it describes "the most secret mysteries of sexual connection."[22] Such poems, Buchanan claims, are in the same vein as the erotic pictures of Simeon Solomon, a young Jewish painter and a lesser member of the Rossetti circle, who was reputed in London literary and art circles to be a homosexual. A few pages earlier Buchanan remarks that Rossetti "seems to have many points in common" with Solomon, a wicked slur which would not be misunderstood by the informed, and certainly not by Rossetti and his friends. Finally, Buchanan assails the awkward prosody

in the poetry of Rossetti, Swinburne, and Morris, pointing especially
to the offbeat accents in Dante Gabriel's "Love-Lily." Then he
applies his own test to all these "fleshly" poets and finds that they
are so easily imitated that many younger poets are writing in their
style and doing better than the originals. Truly great poets, Buchanan avers, are inimitable.

Immediately following the publication of Buchanan's article
there was complete silence, but it was the calm that precedes the
tempest. On October 23, 1871, Swinburne wrote William Rossetti
that Simeon Solomon had written him a note saying that James
Knowles, editor of the *Contemporary*, had told him that Buchanan
had written the article.[23] The same letter expresses Swinburne's
rage and determination that Buchanan be punished; then, abruptly,
he reflects that it might be better to treat him with silent contempt.
The outcome proves that the earlier opinion prevailed and that
the Rossettis and their friends voted for war. But, first, they had
to get the quarry into the open before they could strike at him;
and doing so was achieved by having one of the circle, Sidney
Colvin, publish in the *Athenaeum* for December 9, 1871, an insulting
letter disclaiming that he intended to write an answer to Thomas
Maitland, who, it was said, was really Robert Buchanan, "a per-
tinacious poet and critic" who had "at last done something which
his friends may quote concerning him . . . ."[24] This insult succeeded
better than could have been hoped for: there came two letters
to the *Athenaeum*, one from Buchanan angrily admitting that
the article was his, denying his responsibility for the nom de plume,
and promising that he would republish the article in an expanded
form and under his own name; and one from publisher Strahan
of the *Contemporary* denying by implication that Buchanan was
the author. In its next issue the *Athenaeum* printed both letters and
its own acidulous comment with a broad hint that both Buchanan
and Strahan were liars, and its accusation that Buchanan used the
disguise to praise his own poems.[25]

The same issue of the *Athenaeum* that carried the contradictory
letters contained "The Stealthy School of Criticism," an article of
over two thousand words defending the *Poems*, signed by Dante
Gabriel; but the cumbersome style is marked by long periods,
Latin diction, tedious use of reservations and parenthetical phrases,
and extremely adroit use of the damaging innuendo and the subtle
implication—all of which are much more characteristic of the

polemical writings of William Rossetti than of his more dynamic and forthright brother. The article is cleverly conceived; for, while purporting to be only a defense, it is also a covert attack. He accuses Buchanan of quoting him out of context and of distorting his meaning. Buchanan's charge of sensuality, he points out, rests on four short quotations from *Poems*. These are from "Nuptial Sleep," "The Last Confession," "Eden Bower," and "Jenny." The quoting out of context, he asserts, applies even to "Nuptial Sleep" because, though it is a sonnet and though Buchanan had quoted it in full, a sonnet is really only one link or stanza in the cycle of "The House of Life" sonnets. It should not be judged separately but only in conjunction with all the other sonnets. Second, the lines Buchanan quoted from "Eden Bower" seem to describe a human love embrace, but actually they deal with the love between Lilith, the fabled first wife of Adam, and the serpent. Third, the lines quoted from "The Last Confession" portray a harlot's laugh: certainly, he claims, no fair-minded person should blame him for making it as objectionable as possible. As for "Jenny," Rossetti does not defend it at all or attempt to meet Buchanan's charge of the curious lack of sympathy on the part of the man. He simply says that Buchanan has accused him of plagiarizing "Jenny" from Buchanan's poems, and this charge will not stand up because Rossetti has never read Buchanan's poems.

Of course, Rossetti's defense is full of holes. A sonnet is a complete poem, not a stanza in a longer poem; and Dante Gabriel knew it full well, as his celebrated sonnet, "The Sonnet," makes clear. Also, the lines from "Eden Bower" do describe an evil, sensuous embrace between the serpent, in reality Satan, and the woman Lilith. Furthermore, the lines Buchanan quotes from "The Last Confession" picture a harlot leaning out of a tavern window, a man coming up behind her, seizing her and *"munching her neck with kisses"* while she laughs coarsely. And Buchanan italicizes the quoted words as the particularly objectionable feature of the quotation. Finally, Buchanan does not accuse Rossetti of outright plagiarism in "Jenny"; he simply says that "Jenny" "bears signs of having been suggested" by some of his poems—quite a different matter. In other words, Rossetti had not at all disproved the accusation of sensuality; he had attempted to sidestep it. But in his summary he claims that he has disproved the charge, and I quote it here to show how cleverly the issue is beclouded and obfuscated:

One cannot but feel that here every one will think it allowable merely
to pass by with a smile the foolish fellow who has brought a charge thus
framed against any reasonable man. Indeed what I have said already is
substantially enough to refute it, even did I not feel sure that a fair balance
of my poetry must, of itself, do so in the eyes of every candid reader . . . .
That I may, nevertheless, take a wider view than some poets or critics, of
how much, in the material conditions absolutely given to man to deal with
as distinct from his spiritual aspirations, is admissible within the limits
of Art,—this, I say, is possible enough; nor do I wish to shrink from such
responsibility. But to state that I do so to the ignoring or overshadowing
of spiritual beauty, is an absolute falsehood, impossible to be put forward
except in the indulgence of prejudice or rancour.[26]

Against Buchanan's charge that Rossetti is more interested in
the sound of poetry than in its sense, he retorts that he deals with
many of the same themes as Shakespeare: love turned to hate,
a savage penalty exacted for a lost ideal, the profound problem of
the prostitute in "Jenny," and the analysis of passion in "The
House of Life." Indeed, he says, this accusation is so easy to disprove
that it is obvious Buchanan is seeking to appeal either to people
who had not read Rossetti's poems or to those who are too easily
influenced by any show of authority.

Rossetti's defense has some notable omissions. Nowhere is there
any mention of James Russell Lowell, though Buchanan had quoted
him rather prominently; and it is impossible to believe that the
Rossetti brothers had not read Lowell's article. Neither is there any
mention of Simeon Solomon or of Buchanan's insulting implication
that Dante Gabriel and Solomon had much in common. Likewise,
there is complete silence on the score of Buchanan's charge of the
puffery of Dante Gabriel's friends, especially in the reviews of
Swinburne and Morris. Nor is any reply made to Buchanan's
satire of the irregular prosody of "Love-Lily" and some of the
other poems, though a good defense could have been constructed
by arguing for the charm of irregular music like that of John Donne
and William Blake.

The article concludes by attacking Buchanan on the following
points: that he, a poet, had done a most unethical deed in attacking a
fellow poet; that it was a grudge attack, inspired by rancor and "personal paltriness"; that his use of the pseudonym was in effect don-
ning a mask to do an evil deed; that in the attack he had perverted the
truth so absurdly that no intelligent person could take him seriously.

As in the defense, the statements of the attack do not bear close
scrutiny. There is no canon forbidding a poet to engage in criticism
and, if he sees fit, to point out the faults of another poet. By 1871
Buchanan had published considerable criticism and deserved the
classification of poet-critic. Lowell also was a poet-critic and had
not hesitated to attack both Swinburne and Rossetti. Nor was the
use of the pseudonym a heinous offense. Buchanan denied that he
had had anything to do with it. William Rossetti said he had proof
that Buchanan had been asked to sign the article but had refused.
There is no record of William's ever having produced such proof. Buchanan's letter to the *Athenaeum* of December 16, 1871, implies that
Strahan added the pseudonym, and Strahan never denied it. Nor
was the omission of Buchanan's name a matter of great guilt. While
most of the articles in the *Contemporary* were usually signed,
not all of them were, especially if they were of such a character that
the authors might have suffered from the revelation of their names.
In such cases pseudonyms or anonymous phrases were used. Likewise, it was not unusual for book reviews in the *Contemporary*
to be unsigned.

As to the charge of prejudice and rancor, I do not doubt that
some anger underlay Buchanan's article, but it was not all personal
or malicious. Swinburne's slighting reference to David Gray had
aroused in Buchanan a desire for revenge, as he admitted in a
subsequent letter to Browning. William Rossetti's sneering insult
to Buchanan as a poetaster could only have added fuel to the fire.
But revenge was not the Scotsman's sole motivation; his Victorian
sense of the proprieties was outraged by *Poems*, and he was expressing
his protest as he had against Swinburne's *Poems and Ballads*.
Both books, it seemed to him, represented determined assaults upon
Victorian standards of morality by cynical, depraved poets;
the duty of a true critic was to withstand and expose them. The
Contemporary was exactly the right rampart from which to launch
such a counterattack, for it was a conservative magazine with a
strong religious bias. Many of its articles dealt with religious
questions of the day, nearly always from the orthodox point of
view. It is entirely possible that publisher Alexander Strahan may
have requested Buchanan to write the Fleshly School article and
that this factor may have led Strahan to write his unfortunate
letter to the *Athenaeum* with the implied denial that Thomas Maitland
was Robert Buchanan.

There is not the space in a work of this kind to tell the complete story of the Fleshly Controversy, nor do I intend to do so. Thus far, I have gone into some detail in matters which are basic to an understanding of the main features of the controversy. From here on I shall simply summarize some of the more important elements; lesser matters I shall pass over quickly or omit. In a critical biography such as this one, the prime concern must be to deal only so far with biographical materials as they have a direct relevance to the literature. All else must be considered extraneous.

Early in May, 1872, Buchanan published his book, *The Fleshly School of Poetry and Other Phenomena of the Day*, under his own name. Strahan was the publisher of what turned out to be the magazine article expanded to three times its original size—a hardback of seven chapters, a preface, and notes. It was a most unfortunate publication, for Buchanan went to such absurd lengths and committed so many offenses against good taste and common sense that he seriously impaired his case, which, with a little effort, could have been made formidable. His purpose in the book, like Rossetti's in "The Stealthy School," was twofold—to defend himself and to enlarge his attack upon his foes. The defense was weak, for he failed to point out Rossetti's false assumptions, misstatements, distortions of meaning, and failure to reply to some of the more important charges—as I have already noted.

On the other hand, Buchanan committed some egregious blunders that he should have avoided. In his preface, for instance, he defends the use of "Thomas Maitland" by asserting vaingloriously that it had been employed "in order that the criticism might rest upon its merits and gain nothing from the name of the real writer."[27] Immediately thereafter, he denies the charge of vanity for injecting himself into the imaginary cast of Hamlet by arguing that he had taken the role of Cornelius, who speaks only one line in the play, when he might well have cast himself as Fortinbras or the First Gravedigger. The implication is clear that he felt he was sufficiently important in the current poetical scene to warrant such self-assignment. And indeed he was, but he should not have been the one to say so. It is remarkable that he was completely unaware that he had damned himself out of his own mouth.

In the expanded attack he says he has lately come to London from the Scottish Highlands to find fleshliness on all sides: in the candy shops, in the dance halls, in the theaters, and in fashionable society. The female leg is everywhere, and fleshliness has become epidemic. Its latest assault has come through the poetry of the Pre-Raphaelites. But he finds that fleshliness in literature is not a new phenomenon: it originally came into the pure stream of English literature through the influence of Dante and Boccaccio upon Chaucer and the Elizabethans. It sullied the works of Sir Thomas Wyatt, the Earl of Surrey, Edmund Spenser, John Donne, Shakespeare, and many others. John Milton and William Cowper did much to correct its influence, but it was only with Wordsworth that the evil was finally overcome. It would probably have vanished altogether had there not been a fresh influx of the virus from the works of Charles Baudelaire, brought into England through the efforts of Swinburne. Now it has again attacked in strength through the poetry of Dante Rossetti. In accordance with Rossetti's invitation in "The Stealthy School," he says he has reread the *Poems*, only to find them every bit as bad as he thought them before. The Italian in "A Last Confession" who murders his mistress is, he thinks, "very like our author, for, besides being disagreeably affected, he had a morbid habit of *brooding* over unclean ideas and suspicions . . . ."[28] As for the "House of Life" sonnets, Buchanan suspects "that the sort of house meant should be nameless; but it is probably the identical one where the author found 'Jenny.'"[29]

The book concludes on a milder note than had the article. Buchanan does not believe that Swinburne and Dante Rossetti consciously meant to promote debauchery and immorality through their poetry: "I believe that both Mr. Swinburne and Mr. Rossetti are honest men, pure according to their lights, loving what is beautiful, conscientiously following what inspiration lies within them."[30] They have simply been misled—Swinburne, by his youth and by too much reading of evil French poets; Rossetti, by his "eternal self-contemplation," as well as by imitating "trashy models" and by failing to respond "to the needs and the duties of his time."[31]

Buchanan protests that he himself is no prude, no Philistine who "would emasculate our poets altogether" or "would substitute for passion the merest humanitarian and other 'sentiment.'" Not at all. His favorite ancient author is Catullus; he prefers Shakespeare to Milton, and he would not expunge a line of Chaucer. He loves to read La Fontaine, the novels of Balzac, the "inimitable, yet questionable, pictures of Parisian life" in the poetry of Paul de

Kock. "But Flesh, merely as the Flesh, is too much" for him.[32]
He concludes by wishing there were a "Sultan of Literature" who
could end such foolishness and prevent the poet from being thus
stultified.

In its issue for May 25, 1871, the *Athenaeum* took notice of Buchanan's book by deploring his lack of judgment in republishing
his charges and the ridiculous lengths to which he had gone in
expanding them. It concluded that "malicious friends" must have
advised him to publish the book and quipped: "Mr. Buchanan
tells how the miasmic influence of Italy 'generated madness even
far north as Hawthornden and Edinburgh.' What influences may
have generated so much foolishness even as far north as the Hebrides
we cannot tell; but only that the foolishness is there, and has ended
in a worthless and discreditable treatment of what might have been
made a perfectly just and interesting question of criticism."[33]

The *Saturday Review* agreed with the substance of Buchanan's
charges but lamented his egotism and bad taste in publishing the
book.[34] The *Graphic* took exception to his criticizing the sensuality
of Rossetti and Swinburne and at the same time praising the sensual
poetry of Whitman and Paul de Kock.[35] The reference to Whitman
was to a note in Buchanan's book admitting that the American
bard had written a few lines of indecent verse but insisting that he
was not a fleshly poet.

Buchanan soon learned that the publication of the book had
indeed been a grave error. He asserted that Tennyson, Browning,
Cardinal Manning, and many others were on his side; but no one
entered the lists in his behalf. Such friends of long standing as George
Eliot and George Henry Lewes fell away from him, and he was left
to bear the brunt alone. Many of his magazine contributions of
1872 and his *White Rose and Red* of 1873 were published anonymously to escape the onslaught of his enemies. In 1873 his magazine
work dwindled to almost nothing. Reviews of his signed works
became noticeably more caustic. With some justice he could say
in later years that, if he had not been made of sturdy fiber, he
might have succumbed altogether.[36]

In the meantime, Swinburne published his pamphlet, *Under
the Microscope*, in July, 1872, about two months after Buchanan's
Fleshly book. He did not deign to argue with his foe as Rossetti
had done in "The Stealthy School," but he pelted him with foul
names and insulting implications. Swinburne's error here, as in

the review of Rossetti's *Poems*, was in going too far and in casting aside all restraint. Swinburne never could understand afterward why his pamphlet had not attracted more attention and favorable notice. The answer, I think, is that, after the first few pages of his ranting, he had lost his audience to boredom and disgust.

In *St. Paul's Magazine* for August, 1872, Buchanan riposted with a clever bit of doggerel called "The Monkey and the Microscope." Alluding to the Darwinian theory of evolution, Buchanan joshed Swinburne much as he had in "The Session of the Poets," except that here he sees him as a squeaking, screaming, chittering monkey instead of as a naughty boy.[37] The analogy was just close enough to Swinburne's grotesque appearance and excitable manner when angry to be painful to the victim. After this publication things were quiet along the Fleshly front until 1875, when Swinburne published his *Essays and Studies* with the republication of the essay on "Matthew Arnold's New Poems" and the addition of the very scornful footnote on David Gray that we have already noted. The note could not have failed to raise Buchanan's temperature to the boiling point and to fill him with a fierce desire for revenge on this defiler of graves.

Buchanan's opportunity came in the summer of 1875 with the publication of an anonymous poem, *Jonas Fisher*, which was authored by James Carnegie, the Earl of Southesk, but which had so many of the characteristics of Buchanan's poetry and such fervent preaching against literary and artistic immorality that Swinburne leaped to the conclusion that it was Buchanan's. In the *Examiner* he published four lines of scurrility called "Epitaph on a Slanderer," signing his own name but not identifying the slanderer.[38] A week later an adverse review of *Jonas* contained the speculation that Buchanan was the anonymous poet. Buchanan published a disavowal in the *Athenaeum* on December 4. Swinburne, unconvinced, in the *Examiner* for December 11, satirized the whole business with a letter titled "The Devil's Due," signing it "Thomas Maitland." In this letter Swinburne oversteps the boundaries of libel by referring to Buchanan as "a polypseudonymous libeller" and by accusing him of praising his own writings while throwing dirt on those of others.

Because Buchanan was living in Ireland, it took him some time to enter suit for libel. When he did, he sued the owner of the *Examiner*, P. A. Taylor, for five thousand pounds. The trial began on

Thursday, June 29, 1876, and lasted for three days. Swinburne and the Earl of Southesk were the only witnesses called, though Dante Rossetti trembled lest he also be subpoenaed. The ineffective defense of Swinburne and Taylor was that "The Devil's Due" had only pointed out that Buchanan had written the Fleshly School article under a pseudonym and that in it he had praised his own works and condemned those of others. By a series of questions on these points the defense attorney attempted to force Buchanan to admit these faults. The judge, A. Archibald, protested against such a procedure. In the course of the trial, passages from the Fleshly article, "The Session of the Poets," some of Whitman's poems, and probably some of Swinburne's and Rossetti's poems were read. Judge Archibald asked why Swinburne, the author of the libel, had not been sued instead of Taylor; and the reply of Buchanan's lawyer was especially humiliating to Swinburne. It was that Swinburne was "a man of straw who presumably could not be made to pay up, and therefore they had fallen back on the proprietor of the paper as a scapegoat . . . ."[39] In his charge to the jury, Judge Archibald made it quite clear that he felt that Swinburne should have been sued instead of Taylor, that he agreed that many of the works of the Fleshly School would have been better unwritten, but that Buchanan had only reproduced their harmful effects by frequent and unnecessary quotation in a "sensational essay."[40] The result of this ambivalent statement was that the jury awarded Buchanan a favorable verdict but minimal damages of a hundred and fifty pounds.

The trial ended all published activity in the controversy until the appearance in 1881 of Buchanan's novel of hatred and forgiveness, *God and Man*, with its anonymous dedication "To An Old Enemy" and its verses of apology, obviously addressed to Dante Rossetti:

> *I would have snatch'd a bay leaf from thy brow,*
> *Wringing the Chaplet on an honoured head;*
> *In peace and tenderness I bring thee now*
> *A lily-flower instead.*

> *Pure as thy purpose, blameless as thy song,*
> *Sweet as thy spirit, may this offering be:*
> *Forget the bitter blame that did thee wrong,*
> *And take the gift from me.*

In a later edition published after Rossetti's death, Buchanan named Rossetti as the "Old Enemy"; and he added two more stanzas in the same vein, rejoicing that his book with the apology had been given to Rossetti before his death, and expressing his certainty that, though he and Dante had never met in life, they would know and greet each other at the Last Judgment. Not content even with this, he added a prose paragraph, upbraiding himself for lacking the courage to put Rossetti's name in the original dedication and expressing his regret for having in the first place been so mistaken as to attack Rossetti's "ennobling and refining literary influence . . . ." The entire affair, he thought, was "simply a proof of the incompetency of all criticism, however honest, which is conceived adversely, hastily, and from an unsympathetic point of view . . . ."

Several factors had prompted the apology and the retraction. First, Buchanan in 1881 had recovered his health and mental stability which, in 1871, were still impaired from his breakdown in 1866. Furthermore, Buchanan's wife had been suffering for some time with cancer and was near death, a factor which sharpened his sympathies with his fellow man, especially one like Dante Rossetti, who had some claim upon his commiseration. Rossetti's physical and mental condition had been worsening over a period of several years, for Oswald Doughty makes clear that he had been going downhill since at least 1868 from his increasing indulgence in chloral and alcohol, from his sexual excesses with a procession of women, and from a congenital morbidity, for insanity was prevalent on both sides of his parentage. News of Rossetti's condition reached Buchanan through Hall Caine and probably through Westland Marston, both of whom were friends of Rossetti as well as of Buchanan. Then, too, Buchanan's Owenism and Victorianism, though they forced him to detest any form of pornography and were certainly among the determinants which led him to attack Rossetti and Swinburne, also enjoined upon him a recognition of his fellow man as a brother entitled to his forgiveness and tolerance. All these factors contributed to his sincere, heartfelt apology and retraction. Indeed, Buchanan proved in his essay "A Note on Dante Rossetti," included in his *A Look Round Literature* in 1887, that his apology was not solely sentimental by boldly stating that all love, even the fleshly variety, was the highest human pleasure —so far had he moved with his times under the impact of Ibsenism and Zolaism.

But Buchanan's apology, instead of being accepted in the generous manner in which it was offered, was quickly used against him by his implacable enemies, chief among them being William Rossetti. Although Dante's death took place ten years after the Fleshly article, they pointed to Buchanan as his executioner. Forgotten, glossed over, or minimized were the real causes of Dante Gabriel's troubles, together with the various provocations given Buchanan by William Rossetti and Swinburne. Totally unmentioned was Lowell's attack upon Dante Gabriel a full year before Buchanan's and on much the same grounds. Nor was any notice taken of the covert omission of "Nuptial Sleep" from republications of the *Poems* until 1904, or that the original title given it by Dante Rossetti was "Placata Venere," which can be translated as "the quieted Venus" or "lust appeased." Doughty tells us that this sonnet had been written in 1869 and that its title had been changed to "Nuptial Sleep" in an endeavor to make it more palatable to the Victorian public.[41]

With such omissions and distortions it was not difficult to cast Buchanan in the role of a villain and Dante Rossetti in that of a tragic victim. As long as he lived, William Rossetti continued to insist that Buchanan's attack was a wretched matter inspired only by Dante's success. In the face of formidable evidence to the contrary, William insisted that it was Buchanan's highly vulnerable book of 1872, not the much more defensible *Contemporary* article of 1871, that had been the direct cause of Dante's subsequent misfortunes and torments. This view prevailed because Buchanan, after his apology, could not gainsay it. As the Victorian mind liberalized in the 1880's and 1890's, Buchanan's criticism assumed more and more the character of a manifestation of mid-Victorian prudery. With the passing years Buchanan was convinced that his career had been blasted by the unfair criticism heaped upon him and his literary offerings as a result of the animosities engendered by the controversy. And, indeed, the stigma has stuck to his name like a curse. He continues to be condemned by some contemporary scholars as a man who, for despicable reasons, launched a vile attack upon an innocent poet.

II *The Outspoken Spokesman*

In an article published in 1893, eight years before his death, Buchanan made it clear that he considered literary work to be secondary to his desire to eradicate social evils and to improve the lot of his fellow man.[42] Here again his Owenite heritage motivated him, as did also his Victorian conscience. He spoke out boldly without fear whenever he felt the occasion warranted it, regardless of whom he might offend or of the cost to himself. After 1872 there was no single year of his life that he was not engaged with somebody in some dispute or other. The other conflicts were not so extensive as the Fleshly war, but they are all interesting and involve some principle or conviction that lay close to Buchanan's heart. Since space will not permit covering all these verbal scuffles, I shall deal only with the most important.

Fierce and direct was the attack he launched in an unsigned article in the *Contemporary* for September, 1877, "The Newest Thing in Journalism." He declared open warfare upon four magazines, *Vanity Fair, The World, Mayfair,* and *Truth,* for pandering to a public appetite for scandal and gossip. They did it, he charged, by attacking prominent people through innuendo and suggestion, taking care always to avoid direct statements which might be actionable. He concentrated his fire upon Edmund Yates of the *World* and Henry du Pré Labouchère of *Truth* as the chief offenders. In 1882 Buchanan emerged from anonymity by continuing the attack in his novel *The Martyrdom of Madeline,* where *The World* appears as *The Whirligig; Truth,* as the *Plain Speaker;* Yates, as Yahoo; and Labouchère, as Lagardère. In the novel he shows the injustice done through journalistic scandal-mongering to a virtuous but unfortunate woman. Both the novel and the article are fervent pleas to the public to end such journals through boycott. Since at least three of these magazines lasted well into the twentieth century, Buchanan failed in his immediate purpose. But at least he turned a hard, white light on the nefarious practice of yellow journalism; and he certainly must have embarrassed some of its more flagrant practitioners.

In one of the essays of his *A Look Round Literature,* Buchanan confessed that Thomas Carlyle and his teachings had been his "abomination" from the time that he had first been able to read.[43] Carlyle, according to Buchanan in an earlier work, became so interested in acquiring fame and influence that he sacrificed to this goal any love he might originally have had for his fellow man or any sympathy for his troubles.[44] As a consequence, he finds that Carlyle has "mercilessly brutalised" Burns, Goethe, and Voltaire,

Terror. In the final pages he states his dual purpose: "One half of this book is devoted to proving, with Mill, that individuals have a natural right to free, unfettered, and even eccentric development; while the argument of the other half is that individual development, being often crass, anarchic, selfish, and harmful to Society, has to be carefully watched and qualified by the corporate conscience."[47] The "terror" that he sees approaching is state socialism like that practiced in imperial Germany. It will, he prophesies, take the form of anarchy which, with the aid of science, will "trample down all the rights of minorities, all the privileges of individuals, all the moral differentiation of the human race. No man will breathe freely in his own dwelling. No personal life will grow, upward or downward, its own way. There will be universal legislation, expressed in a creed which shall base the salvation of the State on the destruction of the individual."[48]

To fend off a charge of reversing his lifelong support of Socialism, he differentiates between State Socialism and what he calls "the higher socialism," which guarantees the individual every possible liberty that does not interfere with the rightful liberties of others. Owenism, of course, is higher Socialism; but Fabianism, despite its gentle program of progress through education, is still State Socialism. He and his good friend, George Bernard Shaw, must have had some warm arguments on that score.

It is worth noting that the fear of the coercion of the individual through a combination of militant Socialism and science is precisely the warning sounded by Aldous Huxley in the twentieth century, beginning with his *Point Counterpoint* (1928), his *Brave New World* (1932), and many of his essays and stories through the 1940's and 1950's. State Socialism took the form of Fascism under Hitler and Mussolini; it has become militant Communism in Soviet Russia, China, and many smaller countries; even Great Britain and the United States have been forced to adopt a great deal of Socialism in order to meet the challenges of the twentieth century. Who can doubt that much of Buchanan's prophecy has come to pass?

On the side of defending the masses against the repressions and restrictions of what we call "rugged individualism" today, Buchanan includes in the *Coming Terror* a series of letters originally published in the newspapers. These attack Thomas Henry Huxley for his negative remarks about Socialism. A second series lashes Huxley for his suspicions that General Booth and the Salvation

Army sought to promulgate religion under the guise of charity.
Booth is a good Samaritan, cries Buchanan, while Huxley is a
Pharisee so devoted to upholding "the tyrannies of Force and
convention" that he feels no compassion for his poor brethren.[49]
Another long open letter is addressed to the home secretary, Henry
Matthews, urging him to reverse the decision of the court to imprison
Henry Vizetelly for publishing and selling the works of Émile Zola.
Buchanan insists that he has no love for such writings, but he
charges that such censhorship constitutes a "Latter Inquisition,"
a hand-me-down from Protestant Puritanism, and should be
abolished because it is a gross interference with the natural rights
of mankind.

Several other essays assail Naturalism in literature. Buchanan
finds it guilty of "dissecting woman" and destroying the old chivalric
ideals. The chief offenders are Zola, Flaubert, de Maupassant,
Théophile Gautier, Paul Bourget, Henrik Ibsen, Henry James, and
such approving critics as George Moore, William Archer, and
Andrew Lang. Claiming to subserve the dogma of "Art for Art's
Sake," they seek "to shock and revolt us with the meannesses of
life"; they "assume that those meannesses most abound where
Religion and Morality are most powerful."[50] Buchanan's stand
here was generally consistent with his basic thesis in the Fleshly
Controversy. No one familiar with the growth of Naturalism in
the twentieth century can doubt that its emphasis is upon the animal
aspects of life and character and that its philosophy is largely one of
cynicism and despair.

A humorous aftermath to Buchanan's tilt with the Naturalists
was that Mrs. Lynn Linton, a well-known novelist, hotly disputed
the Scotsman's claim that even a fallen woman should be treated
chivalrously, and not cruelly dissected, as was the habit of the
Naturalists. Such coddling would only result in more working
girls turning to prostitution, she argued, instead of persevering
in lives of virtue. Mrs. Linton had the better of the argument,
which ran its length in the pages of the *Daily Telegraph*, because
she could assume more intimate knowledge of feminine character
than he. Nor could he wheel up the heavy artillery of scorn and
invective without showing himself guilty of the very fault he was
decrying. For the only time in his career, Buchanan retired in silent
chagrin, leaving the lady in possession of the field.

Still other letters to the *Daily Telegraph* took issue with William

E. Gladstone in his view that marriage was so sacred that a second marriage should never be entered into, even after the death of one's partner. Divorce was, of course, unthinkable and impermissible under any circumstances. Not so, argues Owenite Buchanan. Marriage is only sacred and lasting if founded on true love. When marriage is not so founded, or when it has been entered into for selfish reasons, it is a tragic mistake, and its victims should be permitted to dissolve it so as to make what might, perhaps, be a lasting love marriage. Still another essay took Gladstone to task for abandoning Charles Stewart Parnell. Parnell, said Buchanan, was a truly great leader victimized by an unholy alliance between corrupt politics and scandal-mongering journalism; and Gladstone should have known better than to permit himself to be misled by such forces. There is no record of Gladstone's ever having replied to Buchanan. Certainly the prevailing twentieth-century view of marriage and divorce accords more with Buchanan than with Gladstone. As for Parnell, most modern historians regard with regret his fall from Gladstone's favor and the consequent postponement of Irish Home Rule until the twentieth century.

When Buchanan died in 1901, most of the obituarists agreed that he had misused his genius in too many polemics. Plainly their view was that he had stood on the wrong side in his polemics, and that, therefore, his efforts had come to nothing. They failed to perceive the underlying love of freedom, justice, fair play, decency, honesty, and humanity that provided the motivation for all—or nearly all—of his altercations. His commentators should not be too severely censured, for they were only expressing the mind of the times. Social progress in the twentieth century has amply vindicated the polemical Scotsman.

CHAPTER 3

The Reluctant Critic

THE salient feature of Buchanan's work in criticism is his manifest distrust of the critic and the critical function. Here, once again, his basic Owenism is discernible. The image of the critic as an aloof judge, one who sits on high in his tower, who looks down upon the toilers in the fields, who pronounces arbitrary and autocratic judgments upon their labors, was exceedingly repugnant to Buchanan's taste. He stubbornly refused to make obeisance to any critic, no matter how noted or learned. Even the best of them, he thought, were but human beings with human imperfections and critical blind spots; therefore, he thought they should walk humbly and judge meekly, always mindful that their most positive judgments could be grossly in error.

Ironically, Buchanan's earliest journalistic assignments in London were, as we have noted, the writing of critical reviews for the *Athenaeum,* the *Eclectic Review,* and other critical organs. He did not seek such assignments; they were simply the work that was available and that he was forced to accept by stern financial necessity. Such work lessened any respect he might have had for criticism, for he soon learned the extent to which bias entered into reviewing. The works of one's friends, or of his editor or publisher, were praised; those of unpleasing people were condemned; those of neutral writers might get a reasonably fair judgment, though, from the careless fashion in which important reviews were often assigned to neophytes, not necessarily an expert one.

Such experiences Buchanan never forgot, and they undoubtedly had much to do with his strong distrust of criticism. They also had much to do with his lifelong denial that he was a critic or that his critical writings were criticism. He stubbornly maintained that they were but "desultory notes" or "mere impressions," not criticisms. Some justification for his claim lay in the fact that he never went to great pains to expound his critical principles. Likewise, his critical opinions often were not carefully developed in accord with a reasoned critical philosophy. They were flung off in the haphazard fashion that an impulsive poet might use in giving random notions of others. Nevertheless, Buchanan's critical writings were viewed as criticisms by his contemporaries, and probably rightly so. After all, if an opinion is meant to be only an impression, why not keep it oral? If one puts it in writing and prints it for all the world to see, it is criticism and will be taken as such.

Buchanan's critical principles were derived from those of Pope, Wordsworth, and Goethe, as well as from the opinions, prejudices, and predilections of his Victorian times and of his Owenite background. He agreed with Pope that criticism is an art and that the true critic is an artist who must strive to empathize with the work before him if he is to judge it fairly. With Wordsworth, he held that the best poetry concerns itself with humble contemporary life, is couched in simple language, and is exalted by poetic vision. He insisted that the poet must be a seer who can view life in a highly original fashion and who is then so emotionally stirred by his experience that he can express himself in inspired, musical language. This same gift of mystical vision must be the critic's also, said Buchanan, or how can he hope to appreciate the poet's achievement? Above all, the poet, or any literary artist, must be sincere, or the result will be immoral.

Pointing to Goethe's statement in his *Conversations,* that a licentious subject when treated by a genius is not odious, Buchanan expanded the principle and related it to sincerity. A genuine artist like Chaucer, he said, could deal sincerely with an immoral subject and make it moral by the honesty of his treatment; conversely, an insincere artist could render a moral subject immoral by his dishonesty. In this respect, it is well to note Buchanan's consistency, for his attack upon Dante Rossetti's *Poems* was based largely upon the charge of affectation and insincerity. Like Goethe also, the Scotsman viewed literature as a vast, common domain in which literary artists are free to borrow from each other at will. Buchanan carried this concept further and gave it an Owenite flavor by holding that all true poets are worthy of equal praise, though they are not of equal genius; for they are all common laborers in the common vineyard, and each is doing his best according to his abilities. As he phrased it: "In the republic of Poetry, there is no aristocracy; all the citizens are equal by right of a common gift; and it is only those who have never learned what poetry *is,* or what the poetic power and temperament mean, who presume to distinguish impertinently between poet and poet, and to throw around one the purple they deny to the other."[1] But, since Buchanan never did explain his idea of the nature of poetry or of what poetic power and temperament really are, we are left to guess at his rationale for this curious statement. A possible inference from it is that all attempts at discriminatory criticism are futile.

As for the rest, as we have shown in Chapter 2, Buchanan's personal views on such matters as war, religion, and imperialism strongly affected his critical judgments, or "impressions"—as did his Victorian sentiments on chivalrous regard for women, compassion for the poor and oppressed, and insistence upon the dignity of the common man. He found it difficult to praise any literary artist or work which ran counter to his cherished beliefs; he could not withhold his approval where he found agreement. These are only human weaknesses, usually discernible in even the greatest critics, but Buchanan was perhaps more susceptible to them, at least in cases where his emotions were strongly engaged.

Despite such deficiencies, however, many of Buchanan's contemporaries were of the opinion that he had done some very good work in criticism and that, if he had taken it more seriously and had devoted himself to it, he could have been an excellent, possibly even a great, critic.

I   David Gray and Other Essays, Chiefly on Poetry

Buchanan's literary career was barely eight years old in 1868 when he published his first volume of criticism, *David Gray and Other Essays, Chiefly on Poetry*. The preface to this book contains a disclaimer which became characteristic in Buchanan's later critical volumes: "The following Essays, indeed, are prose additions and notes to my publications in verse, rather than mere attempts at general criticism, for which, indeed, I have little aptitude."[2] The preface closes with an extravagant eulogy of "Gray's wonderful poems . . . the truest, purest, tenderest lyrical note that has floated to English ears this half-century," and with a dark reference to "coteries" who had failed to appreciate him because his music was "too low and tender to attract crowds."[3]

The material of the book falls into four categories: the essay on Gray, the exposition of Buchanan's theories of poetry, the application of those theories to others, their application to himself and, finally, to his poems. The titular essay on Gray is clearly the best piece in this collection and is also among the best prose that Buchanan ever achieved. Written in a simple, charming style with complete absence of affectation, it evinces deep sympathy for the subject that brings it very close to poetic prose. There is such a conscious effort to cast a pastoral charm over Gray's pathetic story that we cannot escape the feeling that Buchanan has minimized some of the faults of Gray's querulous nature in order to fit him into the role of the woeful poet.

Three subsequent essays are devoted to Buchanan's theories of poetry. The first, "The Poet, or Seer," in addition to the claim of clairvoyance for the poet that we have already noted, states that the poet's mission is to interpret life to men. To perform this mission, the poet must have sympathy with the poor, as well as great knowledge and culture. Everyday life, says Buchanan, affords many subjects for poetry to the true poet, though many critics do not seem to realize it. Every form of life which can be treated spiritually without the introduction of false elements is suitable to poetry. Universal in scope, poetry is an art that deals with all classes of society, all conditions and aspects of life. The final criterion for evaluating it is the catholicity of its appeal.

The second essay sets forth his views on literary morality. In applying the principles that we have already noted, he finds that Petronius, Juvenal, Fontaine, Jonson, Chaucer, and Swift are moral; George Sand, Congreve, Farquhar, and Aphra Behn are insincere, therefore immoral. Walt Whitman, too, is a moral poet, even in his "Children of Adam," which "simply chronicles acts and functions which, however unfit for art, are natural, sane, and perfectly pure."[4] Despite Whitman's grossness, his repetition without variety, his poor taste, he is a pioneer, rough and crude, creating a new literature. Generations of American poets will follow in his steps.

In his consideration of Whitman, Buchanan shows his true critical acumen. In 1868, the American bard had few friends and even fewer readers who understood and appreciated him. Yet here was a young poet in a foreign land, out of the stream of American thought and idiom, who not only comprehended his genius, but also gauged correctly his place in American poetry. Buchanan's estimation of Whitman did not change substantially throughout his life. His critical judgment has been seconded by the verdict of posterity.

The third essay, "The Student and His Vocation," is a rather rambling discussion of what constitutes a true student. He is one, says Buchanan, like Plato, Comte, and Spinoza—one who surrounds himself with solitude so that he might better seek eternal truth. Yet he is also one who, when the need arises, abandons his study, descends to the marketplace, and becomes a leader of men. Men revere him because they intuitively sense his sincerity and love for his fellow man. But the least sign of contempt for the people betrays the false student, the charlatan who despises his vocation. Such false students are Thomas Carlyle and Matthew Arnold—Carlyle, because the sole aim of his life has been to gain personal influence, and because of his strongly expressed scorn for the Negro and for the mass of mankind; Arnold, because he was merely a vain, self-centered product of the schools, with very little knowledge of the real world or concern for the problems of mankind.

The final essay, "On My Own Tentatives," was a blunder; for in it Buchanan discusses, defends, and praises his own verse. It is an excellent illustration of that peculiar insensitivity to the inevitable reactions of others that he inherited from his father and that made his father one of the most hated of the Owenite missionaries. It is nearly always unwise for a literary artist to talk back to his critics, and it was especially so in this case because Buchanan not only defended his verse but found it good. In the three volumes of poetry he has so far published, he says, he has tried to show that actual contemporary life affords a far better material for the poet than does the material of the past. He firmly believes that "the further the poet finds it necessary to recede from his own time, the less trustworthy is his imagination, the more constrained his sympathy, and the smaller his chance of creating true and durable types for human contemplation." Then he adds complacently: "The success of my writings with the simple people may be no sign of their possessing durable poetic worth, but it at least implies that I have been labouring in the right direction."[5]

After this statement he proceeds to a discussion of criticism of his poetry, giving each specific adverse criticism and then attempting to rebut it. He closes with a minute examination of some of his poems, explaining why he wrote them as he did and what they were meant to convey. In all likelihood he meant the essay to be nothing more than an exposition and illustration of his own poetic method and technique—a sort of manual for other young poets and, mayhap, critics. But Buchanan was not long in discovering how widely he had missed the mark. To a man, the reviewers came down on him with heavy satire for his vanity, for the dogmatic tone of many of his criticisms, and for what most of them saw as a certain implication that he believed himself endowed with the special powers of a critical seer. They were irritated by the casual manner in which he had dealt with Sir Walter Scott, William Thackeray, George Crabbe, Robert Southey, and even Sir Francis Bacon. Most of them praised the excellent writing in the essay on Gray. A few, notably the *Athenaeum* and the *Contemporary Review,* conceded that, despite his evident faults, he displayed genuine critical acumen.[6]

II *A Matched Pair of Wooden Horses*

Shortly after the publication of his Fleshly article in October, 1871, Buchanan became convinced that he was a marked man and that the Rossettis and their friends—many of whom held key positions as critics and reviewers on leading magazines and newspapers—would blast anything of his printed under his name. As he phrased it: "'All the cockney bastions of criticism were swarming with sharpshooters on the lookout for the 'd——d Scotchman' who had dared to denounce Logrolling."[7] His biographer and sister-in-law, Harriet Jay, says that he was "relentlessly pursued" by a "band of Mohawks" who drove him into anonymity, and that "when the story is told of how they have laboured to discredit him . . . it will form one of the most humiliating episodes in the literary history of our generation."[8]

The story has not yet been told, but the body of it can now be pieced together with the aid of fact and conjecture so that it forms a coherent tale. It is more amusing than tragic, and whatever humiliation it created was felt by Buchanan's foes, not by their intended victim. It supports Buchanan's thesis that criticism is so closely interconnected with and influenced by the critic's personal bias that errors in judgment are inescapable.

Buchanan sized up his opponents as being so eager to come at him that their very impetuosity could be used against them. If he could concoct a scheme to expose their bias and critical ineptitude, he could so discredit them that they would be objects of ridicule. Such a stratagem readily occurred to him: he would publish two poetical works simultaneously, or almost so. One, signed with his name, would be a serious work of as high quality as he could make it. The other would be anonymous, would be camouflaged in matter and style to appear as much unlike Buchanan's previous verse as possible and as much like the work of some popular poet as Buchanan's imitative abilities could fashion it, but it would be mere doggerel. If his assailants fell into the trap by condemning the good work and praising the farce, he could then expose them to the world and enjoy their chagrin.

He was not long in putting his plan into effect. The serious work, *The Drama of Kings,* was a book-length poem examining the careers of Napoleons I and III in order to determine whether there was a God and whether there was concrete evidence of His intervention in the affairs of men during the Napoleonic Wars and the Franco-Prussian War. The issue is still in some doubt at the conclusion of some four hundred and fifty pages of somewhat noisy verse, for Buchanan has been unable to find any clear evidence of the Almighty in the bloody campaigns of the Bonapartes. Appearing in the latter half of November, 1871, little more than a month after the Fleshly articles in the *Contemporary Review,* the *Drama of Kings* was a hastily composed, ill-fated attempt to make poetic capital out of the recently concluded strife across the Channel. To it Buchanan appended a "Note on Mystic Realism," asserting that the *Drama* represented an innovation in modern literature because it utilized the form and manner of Greek drama in depicting great historical events. He concluded with a plea for a patient hearing for his epic, and then he dourly observed that he had little hope of getting it— certainly poor salesmanship unless his real intent was to invite adverse criticism.

The second work, the farcical *St. Abe and his Seven Wives/A Tale of Salt Lake City,* was published anonymously one month later in the latter half of December, 1871. The flimsy melodramatic plot centers about the troubles experienced by "St." Abe Clewson, a Mormon elder, with his six older wives when he marries a young and beautiful seventh. The story ends with his flight to New England with the young wife and his bequeathing the six belligerent older ladies to Brigham Young in a letter delivered after Abe's departure.

Poor as the story is, Buchanan's manner of telling it is even worse. The viewpoint is author-observer; the prosody is rhymed couplets, varying from iambic tetrameter to iambic heptameter; it is doggerel, not poetry. As an example, we cite the opening scene that describes Buchanan's stagecoach ride to Salt Lake:

> *"Grrr!" shrieked the boss, with teeth clench'd tight,*
> *Just as the lone ranche hove in sight,*
> *And with a face of ghastly hue*
> *He flogg'd the horses till they flew*
> *As if the devil were at their back,*
> *Along the wild and stony track.*
> *From side to side the waggon swung,*
> *While to the quaking seat I clung.*
> *Dogs bark'd; on each side of the pass*
> *The cattle grazing on the grass*
> *Raised heads and stared; and with a cry*
> *Out the men rush'd as we roll'd by.*[9]

On other counts also *St. Abe* leaves much to be desired. The humor is so forced that it often becomes grotesque. Neither the story, the characters, nor the setting has immediacy. Buchanan deliberately and prudently shied away from the specific in dealing with his material. His West is any place with a winding road, hills, cattle, and dogs. Salt Lake City shines in the distance and could as well be Camelot. In details of dialect, his misconception is often ludicrous, for the stage-driver speaks like a Cockney. The whole work is so very poor that any critic who praised it would stand convicted either of puffery or of utter lack of critical discernment.

But for Buchanan's purpose his wooden horse was well conceived and executed. It was an American story set in America, and Buchanan's enemies were aware that he had never been any nearer to America than the English coast. Also, while Buchanan's earlier poetic works had been highly serious, *St. Abe* was a humorous satire on Mormonism. Furthermore, Buchanan through his Fleshly article had taken the mantle of a guardian of the public morals, but in *St. Abe* he treats of polygamy and free love with a salacious relish that is excellent camouflage. Likewise, he went to great lengths to convince his foemen that *St. Abe* was the work of an American poet and that the poet was none other than James Russell Lowell. In his dedication to Chaucer, he speaks of England as "the Mother-land" and his dateline for the dedication was "Newport, October, 1871." Lowell's satirical *Biglow Papers* had been sufficiently popular in England to run through nine editions before 1872, and *St. Abe* employed much of the tone, the manner,

the prosody, and the dialect of the *Biglow Papers*. The dedication
to Chaucer was shrewdly contrived, for Lowell's *Conversations
on Some of the Old Poets* published in 1845 expresses his admiration
for Chaucer. Finally, it would have been in character for Lowell
to publish *St. Abe* anonymously because both his *Fable for Critics*
and his *Biglow Papers* had originally been published thus. If Lowell
could be indicated as the author of *St. Abe,* it would be assured of
a favorable critical reception. In 1871, the British were anxious to
repair their breach with the United States that had come about
during the Civil War; and Lowell was one of the most popular
American men of letters.

The result was all that Buchanan could have hoped for. The
critical press belabored the *Drama* with ferocity. The *Athenaeum*
devoted more than four columns to a strongly negative review in
which it pointed out that he was imitating his arch-enemy,
Swinburne.[10] The *Academy* sneered that he had failed to fulfill
his early promise to become "the costermonger's Wordsworth"
and that his later works proved that he was "essentially a spas-
modic poet."[11] The *London Quarterly* found in the *Drama* "no
dearth of materials that indicate the hand of a word-monger rather
than the head and heart of a poet."[12] The *Graphic* suspected that
his "Note" showed that he considered his readers stupid for failing
to comprehend his writings,[13] and the *British Quarterly* acidly
recommended shortening the poem by at least a hundred pages.[14]

In sharp contrast was the chorus of praise that greeted *St. Abe*.
The *Athenaeum* found the description of Salt Lake City and the
Mormons to be especially good.[15] The cleverness of the poem and
the satire of the Mormons delighted the *London Quarterly*.[16] The
British Quarterly strongly suspected Lowell to be the poet of *St.
Abe* and declared the quality of the poetry to be superior to that of
Hans Breitmann, Bret Harte, or Joaquin Miller. Like the *Athenaeum,*
it singled out as especially meritorious the "characteristic scenes of
Mormon life."[17] The *Graphic* plunged headlong into the trap: on
the same page and immediately below its unfavorable review of the
Drama quoted above, it said: "St. Abe and His Seven Wives . . .
belongs to a very different class of poetry. The author has one
advantage over Mr. Buchanan, that his muse deals in realism
mixed, and nobody need be in any doubt as to what he means. . . .
Such vigorous, racy, determined satire has not been met with for
many a long day, certainly not in verse."[18] *Temple Bar* carried

this strain to an even higher key. After agreeing that *St. Abe* must be the work of Lowell and that it was clearly one of the best poems of the season, it concluded with a remark that Buchanan quoted gleefully in later years: "Truly, if America has more than one writer who can write in such a rich vein of satire, humour, pathos, and wit as we have here, England must look to her laurels."[19]

Buchanan had every reason to be pleased with his "haul." Although he must have recognized that the merits of his *Drama* were open to debate, the demerits of *St. Abe* were beyond question. He did not, however, immediately expose his victims—and for readily understandable reasons. Ill and in need of money, he was gratified to see that *St. Abe*, aided by the favorable reviews, was selling better than anything he had published for years. For its creator to have revealed that it was a spurious poem, a hoax, would surely have been to kill its sale and to stop the flow of money into his empty pockets. Much wiser would it be to forgo his revenge— at least temporarily—come out with a second venture of the same general character, and reap a double harvest. An added advantage of such a course would be to establish the culpability or incapability of his critical antagonists beyond argument.

This was precisely what Buchanan did. His *White Rose and Red* appeared during the first two weeks of August, 1873. Another melodrama of the American West, it deals with a Maine farmer youth who goes to the Far West, is captured by Indians, secretly marries the daughter of the chief, gets free of the Indians and returns to Maine, marries a white girl, and settles down to the life of a farmer, forgetting the Indian girl and his promise to return to her. But she has not forgotten him. With her child in her arms she wanders over rivers, mountains, and plains, in scenes reminiscent of *Uncle Tom's Cabin,* until she comes at last to her husband's home in Maine. There she obligingly dies from exhaustion, leaving her child to its father and his white wife—an excellent arrangement because their marriage has been childless. Buchanan supplemented this threadbare plot by repeating most of the devices that had been successful in palming off *St. Abe* as an American work, again with indications of Lowell as the author. The same prosody, the same dialect, the same easy tolerance of sensuality and immorality— all are in evidence. This work is also anonymous, the title page containing the information that it was "by the author of St. Abe."

Once again the bag of reviewers was eminently successful, and the sale of the book highly gratifying to the Scottish strategist. The *Athenaeum,* the *British Quarterly,* the *Illustrated News,* and even the usually astute *Spectator* marshaled platoons of encomiastic phrases to express their approbation, most of them singling out the ludicrously spurious descriptions of American scenes and characters for especial praise as being vivid and authentic.

As early as October, 1873, less than two months after the publication of *White Rose,* the secret began to leak out with the announcement in the *Westminster Review* that the author of the poem was not an American, although "his poetry has a wonderful likeness to that of the new American school."[20] This was followed in November, 1873, with an article on Buchanan in the *Contemporary* by George Barnett Smith, suggesting that Buchanan had done both *St. Abe* and *White Rose.* Since Alexander Strahan, publisher of the *Contemporary* had also published both *St. Abe* and *White Rose,* the suggestion had almost the weight of an official announcement.

Except that Buchanan's health was still poor and his finances were even worse, there is no ready answer as to why he did not appear in print late in 1873 or early in 1874 with the exposé of his enemies. Certainly the cat was out of the bag, and the time was ripe to let the world know of the success of his scheme. He could be certain that Smith's article had made clear to his foes how he had tricked them. They would be waiting in daily apprehension for Buchanan's article to hold them up to public ridicule. Perhaps he considered it more refined torture to keep them in an agony of suspense than to give them the coup de grâce. Furthermore, not all the reviewers and reviewing organs were inimical to Buchanan. Some of them, like Richard Holt Hutton of the *Spectator,* were long-time friends. Exposure would have hurt them as well as the others. For whatever reasons, the article was never published.

Not until 1882, in his novel *The Martyrdom of Madeline,* did Buchanan treat himself to the delicious pleasure of ribbing his critical adversaries. He did it by introducing a scene in which several critics are gathered together in an artist's salon, discussing the merits of a poem, *Lily and Rue,* recently published. All agree that it is of high excellence until they learn, to their consternation, that it is the work of a man they hate, a cantankerous Scotsman named MacAlpine. The news is so disturbing that the editor of the *Megatherium,* a leading critical journal, staggers from the room.

The others change their opinions abruptly, now finding that *Lily and Rue* is worthless drivel.

Lily and Rue is, of course, *White Rose;* MacAlpine is Buchanan; and the *Megatherium* is the *Athenaeum*. One of Buchanan's friends at the gathering reminds the chagrined critics that this is the second time the Scotsman has hoodwinked them. He adds a cutting remark that their vaunted critical insight is nothing but bias: they can see nothing but faults in the works of their enemies; nothing but virtues in those of their friends.

Thus Buchanan had a partial measure of his revenge at last. Most of the London literary world would know the full import of the scene in the novel; many of them would know the identities of the befooled reviewers. The reviewers themselves would most certainly know how they had been diddled by "the damned Scotchman." Best of all, from Buchanan's viewpoint, they must suffer in silence; they could not answer him back directly without further publicizing their own sorry predicament. It had been a most successful venture. As his friend Archibald Stodart-Walker later remarked, Buchanan in *St. Abe* and *White Rose* had "risked a fall with the Philistine, and succeeded even beyond his most ambitious hope."[21] To his own satisfaction at least, Buchanan felt that he had demonstrated the hopeless bias of contemporary criticism.

III   *Aftermath*

Buchanan's view of criticism showed a rapid pejoration after *St. Abe* and *White Rose*. It is apparent in his second volume of criticism, *Master-Spirits* (1873). Current criticism, he exclaims, is at such a low ebb that it is a mistake to dignify it by the term. It is nothing more than an impression given by one man, often so strongly biased that his opinions are worthless. Too often, he adds, the so-called critic is an incompetent youth who is beyond his intellectual depth in the works he is attempting to judge.

His denigration of criticism continued in his third critical volume, *A Look Round Literature,* (1887); and he cites his own attack upon Dante Rossetti as an example of negative bias that so distorted the vision of the critic that he could not discern true beauty. He predicts that the "literary Inquisition" will vanish as had the religious one, but it will take time. Then, with an obvious glance at his own predicament, he grimly reflects that the reward in store for any original writer is "the privileges of martyrdom," that "criticism flourishes on the grave of imagination," and that the leading contemporary critics are but "cicerones" attempting to imitate Goethe.[22] His climactic conclusion is that all human attempts to judge the fruits of genius are as prone to error as efforts to judge the human soul: "I can advance no scientific reason for seeing a great genius in Robert Browning, or a fine painstaking talent in George Eliot, for thinking George Meredith almost alone in his power of expressing personal passion, and Walt Whitman supreme in his power of conveying moral stimulation. I can take a skeleton to pieces scientifically, but not a living soul."[23]

The assumption that the work is the product of the soul and therefore unjudgeable by even a talented critic is one that most critics would dispute. The soul enters into a great work, they would allow, but so does the brain. Any work of art is at least partially subject to the established rules and the established practices of that art form, as well as to comparison with other great works in that medium. And it is most certainly subject to the judgments of successive generations of mankind. But, by the same token, most critics would admit that any work of true genius is certain to have some mystery about it that nobody can penetrate or explain. For twenty-eight hundred years, for instance, Homer's *Odyssey* has been hailed as one of the peaks of world literature, but nobody has ever fully explained why, and nobody ever will.

Buchanan's conclusion from his nearly three decades of wrestling with the whole matter of criticism can be arrived at by inference: no one should indulge in criticism unless he is endowed with genuine critical genius. Even then, the critic should walk humbly, always conscious of his own limitations, his own human frailty. He should not hand down his judgments as though they were infallible pontifications. Indeed, he should not call them judgments; he should, like Buchanan, style them as impressions; for that is all that they really are. He should always criticize in the spirit of brotherhood and with the sole desire of being helpful—and he should always be mindful that he is only one man seeking to understand and evaluate the artistic work of another, and that both the work and its creator partake of a large element of impenetrable mystery.

This conclusion, of course, applies only to honest critics of good will. Dishonest critics of the kind who had condemned Buchanan's *Drama* because they hated him and who had been misled by puffery into extolling his *St. Abe* and *White Rose* should be hunted out and cried down. Too many contemporary critics were of this character, he observed gloomily in his last volume of criticism, *The Coming Terror* (1891). For that matter, the whole world had worsened since the days of his youth, and dire things lay ahead unless a radical change occurred. London in 1890, he says solemnly, is in the same general state of decadence as Rome was in the days of Juvenal. The old critics, now gone, have been succeeded by a young Cockney clique who completely dominate contemporary criticism and use it to praise their friends and persecute their foes. Among their prime foes are Robert Buchanan and all other writers who dare to think for themselves and who do not subscribe to the prevailing philosophical patterns.

Chief among these young upstart critics are George Moore, novelist, essayist, critic, and esthete; Andrew Lang, poet, folklorist, journalist, and critic; and William Archer, drama critic, translator, and biographer. With all three of these Buchanan had sharp differences: with Moore, because he called himself a successor to Rossetti and Swinburne and expressed his contempt for Buchanan; with Lang, because he hailed Robert Louis Stevenson as the equal of Sir Walter Scott; with Archer, because he ridiculed the Victorian melodrama and extolled the works of Henrik Ibsen, which, in Buchanan's view, dissected woman and destroyed the ideal of chivalry.

The Coming Terror closes with a final section entitled "Final Words," in which Buchanan stubbornly reiterates his faith that, despite the efforts of false critics, good literature will last; but "the houses of mud and sand will crumble away, and the ephemeral names written on the shore will be effaced."[24] Mankind will likewise persevere through the approaching time of terror to achieve a new and beautiful time of peace and happiness. Buchanan's desperate insistence leads us to suspect that he was only whistling past the cemetery of his own youthful dreams.

His pessimism is even heavier in an autobiographical article, "My First Books," which appeared in 1893 as one of a series by various British men of letters. He is completely negative toward criticism and the whole profession of literature as he viewed it in the latter days of the Victorian age. Almost from his earliest days in London, he says, he had recognized "the whole unmistakable humbug and insincerity of the literary life."[25] He earnestly advises

the young not to undertake literature as a profession because of
its harmful effects:

With a fairly extensive knowledge of the writers of my own period, I can
honestly say that I have scarcely met one individual who has not deteriorated
morally by the pursuit of literary Fame. For complete literary success among
contemporaries, it is imperative that a man should either have no real
opinions, or be able to conceal such as he possesses, that he should have one
eye on the market and the other on the public journals, that he should
hum-bug himself into the delusion that book-writing is the highest work in
the Universe, and that he should regulate his likes and dislikes by one law,
that of expediency. If his nature is in arms against anything that is rotten
in Society or in Literature itself, he must be silent. Above all, he must lay
this solemn truth to heart, that when the World speaks well of him the World
will demand the *price* of praise, and that price will possibly be his living
Soul.

With greater specificity and heavier irony, Buchanan tallies the
"do's" and "dont's" of literary prosperity: "the hall-mark of
contemporary success is perfect Respectability. It is not respectable
to be too candid on any subject, religious, moral, or political. It
is very respectable to say, or imply, that this country is the best of
all possible countries, that War is a noble institution, that the
Protestant Religion is grandly liberal, and that social evils are only
diversified forms of social good."

He illustrates his attack by claiming that three-fourths of
Tennyson's success was due to his representing the viewpoint of
the English public school and of middle-class education, but Walt
Whitman was neglected by contemporary criticism because he
dissented from prevailing patterns of thought. George Eliot enjoyed
great popularity because she always, in her novels, conformed to
current views; but Charles Reade languished in comparative
obscurity because he had dared to dissent. Buchanan does not say
so in so many words, but the implication is unmistakable that he
himself is a prime victim of critical disapproval because he has
always dared to speak the truth, regardless of whom it offended or
of the consequences of the offense. In his own words, he had refused
to pay the price of the world's praise.

Besides Buchanan, twenty-one other English authors of the day
published articles in the *Idler's* "My First Book" series. Among
them were Walter Besant, Grant Allen, Morley Roberts, Marie
Corelli, Rudyard Kipling, Hall Caine, A. Conan Doyle, H. Rider

Haggard, Jerome K. Jerome, and Robert Louis Stevenson. The articles were gathered into a book and published in 1897.[26] No other author in the series writes so harshly of the profession as Buchanan, although some of them—notably Grant Allen, Morley Roberts, and Marie Corelli—complain sufficiently about the unfairness of publishers and reviewers to indicate that Buchanan's charges were not without substance. There is no doubt that England in the 1890's was still laboring under many Victorian taboos; that many of Buchanan's poems, novels, and essays had violated some of these taboos; and that he had brought down upon his own head the angry recriminations of both public and press. But it is equally certain, as the *Idler* article implies, that in the later stages of his career his devotion to literature waned as his interest in social problems increased. The result was that some of his later works were of such poor quality that no competent critic could fail to find fault with them. Consequently, between Buchanan's complaint against the critics and theirs against him, the truth lies somewhere in the middleground.

CHAPTER 4

The Celtic Glamor

WHEN we glance over the totality of Buchanan's poetry published posthumously in the two volumes of his *Complete Poetical Works* in 1901, we are impressed with the sheer bulk of his production. Reviewing the publication, the anonymous reviewer for the *Academy* said he would not be surprised to learn that Buchanan was the poet of the "greatest number of lines" of the nineteenth century.[1] That this dubious compliment was not without foundation, a comparison of Buchanan's output with that of so prolific a poet as Browning shows. Buchanan's two volumes contain a total of 966 double-column pages. The Student's Cambridge Edition of *Browning's Complete Poems* has 1,007 pages with approximately the same number of lines a page as Buchanan's, but it also has prose introductions and analyses for most of the poems. Since Buchanan's two volumes contain only his poetry and since large sections of his *Drama of Kings,* as well as many scattered pieces are missing, it is reasonable to assume that the poetic production of the two Roberts was equal in quantity. And, when we remember that Browning's life-span was seventeen years longer, Buchanan's output is all the more remarkable. Had he done nothing else, his poetry would stand as evidence that he had not buried his talents in the earth. It is evidence also of the high seriousness with which he regarded his poetic career. He insisted that he was a poet, not a critic, not a novelist, not a playwright, though the demands of his times forced him into these literary channels. He pursued them reluctantly and, especially in the novel and the drama, with considerable financial success. But his attitude toward them was almost one of careless indifference. He could spin off a potboiling novel or a melodrama in great haste to pay the butcher or the baker, but he always took his poetry seriously, except, perhaps, in the case of *St. Abe, White Rose*, and a few other casual pieces.

His low view of prose fiction and the drama, especially the melodrama, was not uncommon in Victorian England. Sir Walter Scott, Charles Dickens, and William Thackeray had done much to elevate the novel to literary respectability, but it was still regarded by intellectuals as having the taint of vulgarity. As for the melodrama, it was designed as entertainment principally for the uneducated; and anybody who wrote such fare was considered as little better than a literary hack. Buchanan blamed his times for forcing him to demean himself to write novels and melodramas. He speaks angrily of Robert Browning's sneering at him as a "writer of plays," and protests that he had no option except starvation.[2] So low had the demand for poetry fallen that nobody but a Tennyson or a Browning could make a living thereby, but the novel and the play were in such popular esteem that even a man of mediocre talent could win rich rewards from them. Buchanan used the rich rewards to support himself and his family while he devoted his major efforts to his poetry.

Buchanan was an intensely personal poet and, true to his own critical principles, was profoundly interested in the contemporary scene. His verse records his reactions to the flow of life about him— his convictions, his protests, his dreams, his deepest emotions, his profoundest inspirations. In it, we can readily discern such Owenite influences as compassion for the poor, scorn for the wealthy and the religiously bigoted, hatred of tyrants and imperialism, a passionate belief in the brotherhood of man, and the recurring dream of an earthly utopia. Evident too are such Victorian strains as a love of nature, a belief in the ideality of true love, a conviction of the upward trend of progress, a chivalrous regard for woman, a sentimental sympathy for the unfortunate and the weak, and, always, nagging doubts and fretful concern about the premises of Christianity. Lastly, Buchanan did not forget his native land. His Scottish poems deal mostly with the penury and pathos of Scottish peasant life, enlivened at intervals with native humor. The Scottish poems contain some of his best songs and some of his most inspired descriptions of nature.

In quest of his own poetic style and domain, Buchanan ran through a gamut of imitations of other poets. Here again his selection of models was influenced by his Owenite traditions, for unmistakable traces of such older bards as Burns, Shelley, and Wordsworth —all in high favor with the Owenites—are evident in his first poetic efforts. The Keatsian influence is there also in the limpid beauty of some of the early lyrics. But, gaining confidence in his developing powers, Buchanan broadened his scope to imitate some of his contemporaries. There is the dramatic monologue, "Fra Giacomo," which owes much to Browning, while his first published volume, *Undertones*, deals with classical themes in the manner of Tennyson's early poems on such subjects. The first volume of Scottish poems, *Idylls and Legends of Inverburn* (1865), returns to Wordsworth, though here and there a new note appears that is Buchanan's. The *London Poems* of 1866, though they exhibit traces of the hasty composition that was becoming his habit, offer clear evidence that the fledgling poet was now learning to rely on his own wings. His *The Book of Orm* of 1870 had a Wordsworthian touch in its subtitle announcing that it was a "prelude to the epic"; but the imitative apprenticeship was clearly over. Henceforth, Buchanan, though he might not soar so high as some of the eagles he had imitated, was flying in his own fashion.

I   *Poems Classical and Medieval*

Near the close of 1863 Buchanan's maiden volume of poetry, *Undertones*, was published by Moxon and Company. Although he continued to use classical themes occasionally in his later verse, this was his first and last volume devoted largely to such materials. There was nothing unusual in such imitations, for, like many other young British poets, his education had centered around a study of the classics; and when he came to write his own verse, he naturally turned to the classical models he had studied in detail.

The poems are set in a personalized framework of the poet's prologue and epilogue. The first, "To David in Heaven," is to David Gray; and the second, "To Mary on Earth," is to Buchanan's wife. Both poems pose significant questions: the first seeks to know the meaning of life; the second pleads for assurance of a fitting reward to the poet for his labors. The other poems—nineteen in all—deal with familiar figures of classical mythology. The theme common to all of them is the discontent of the pagan gods with their labor and its inadequate reward, and these sullen mutterings are the "undertones" of the title of the volume.

Buchanan's prologue, "To David in Heaven," sets the melancholic key for the entire book. Sitting in his London room on a moonlit night in summer, he asks if his quest for poetic greatness is in vain. Is he, too, pursuing an empty dream in this city of broken dreams?

> *Do I dream, I wonder?*
> *As, sitting sadly under*
> *A lonely roof in London, thro' the grim square pane I gaze?*
> *Here of you I ponder,*
> *In a dream, and yonder*
> *The still streets seem to stir and breathe beneath the white moon's rays.*
> *By the vision cherish'd,*
> *By the battle bravéd,*
> *Do I but dream a hopeless dream, in the city that slew you, David?*[3]

This query he answers toward the end of the poem with the hope that even the most insignificant poet, if he labors faithfully, may ultimately be united with the great poets in that "poets' corner" of heaven where "human power and failure/ Are equalized for ever/ And the one great Light that haloes all is the passionate bright endeavour!"[4] This statement, of course, is a poetic rendering of his critical principle that all true poets belong to a sort of artistic democracy rather than to a feudal hierarchy

Most of the ideology of his later verse is present in the *Undertones,* though often limned in faint lines. The dogma of Comte and Owen that all formal religions would ultimately become obsolete is adumbrated in Pan's prophecy in the poem "Pan" that an eternal law shall one day hurl all the gods from Olympus and elevate Pan (mankind) to triumph. The prophecy is fulfilled in the "Swan-Song of Apollo" when Christ appears with His cross. Nowhere is there any mention that Christianity, too, would pass, possibly because prudence forbade its inclusion thus early in Buchanan's career.

Imitations of Wordsworth, Keats, Shelley, Browning, and Tennyson are readily observable in *Undertones.* Buchanan's prosody also follows well-established patterns. Iambic tetrameter and pentameter predominate, with a sprinkling of trimeter and dimeter in the lighter themes. His rhyme schemes are simple, with liberal use of the couplet and of the *a,b,a,b,* or *a,b,b,a,* rhymed stanzas. The rhymes are usually exact and traditional. All in all, *Undertones is* clearly the work of an earnest, intelligent young man striving to master his art by following carefully selected models. Like most first volumes, it does not lack crudities, extravagances of thought and diction, and instances of poor taste and judgment; but it also has strains of music that explain why the reviewer for the *British Quarterly,* though he could discern little originality in the classical imitations, believed that Buchanan revealed a true talent that at times enabled him to ascend to "the upper regions of his art."[5]

Buchanan's medieval poems were never gathered into a single volume but were published in various magazines during his early years in London. Strongly imitative and reminiscent of the medieval verse of Tennyson and Browning, they divide easily into two genres: Arthurian stories like Tennyson's *Idylls of the King,* and anti-Catholic dramatic monologues in the vein of Browning's "Soliloquy of the Spanish Cloister" and "The Bishop Orders His Tomb at St. Praxed's Church." Very few of these are included in Buchanan's *Complete Poems* of 1901, possibly because he, or Harriett Jay, deemed them unworthy. The best of the Arthurian poems is "Merlin and the White Death," published in *Once a Week* in 1864.[6] Its excellence lies chiefly in its powerfully dramatic rendering of a charming tale in simple, beautiful verse. After the manner of Keat's "La Belle Dame Sans Merci," this story recounts the efforts of the aged Merlin to break the spell of the Lady of the Lake and to free the knights imprisoned in her underwater cave. Merlin is spurred on by an old legend promising eternal youth to the mortal who could thwart the enchantress. But, alas! he is himself overcome; for, when he goes by night to her lake to cast a spell upon her, she rises from the waters and so bewitches him with her beauty that he longs for death so that he may become one of her victims.

Buchanan's later success with the drama is foreshadowed in his medieval dramatic lyrics. Clearly evident in them are his keen sense of the dramatic; his ability to suit speech to character; his skillful blending of scene, character, and story; and his subtle suggestion of interplay between characters. He had obviously studied his Browning thoroughly. A good example of his work in this direction is included in the "Early Poems" of the *Complete Poems,* though I have been unable to find it elsewhere. Set in Venice and entitled "Fra Giacomo," the poem has as monologuist a Renaissance Italian husband who adroitly informs his guest, the painter-monk Fra Giacomo, that he has discovered that the monk has seduced his dead wife, who lies upstairs in her coffin, poisoned by her vengeful husband. When Fra Giacomo rises in fear and horror, the husband taunts him that the wine he has been drinking has also been poisoned and that his death is imminent. To make doubly sure of his death, however, the husband leaps upon him in a trice, whips out his dagger, and crying, "Take this!—and this!—and this!" dispatches him, and then calmly bids a servant to cast his body into the canal below.[7]

II Scottish Poems

Despite Buchanan's and his father's many differences with their Scottish countrymen, the poet was proud of his ancestry and background. Although on his mother's side he was at least partially English, he seldom makes mention of the fact; but he not infrequently refers in his writings to his Highland descent through his father. It is not surprising, therefore, to find him devoting some attention to Scottish themes in his verse. Most of the Scottish poetry is contained in two volumes, *The Idylls and Legends of Inverburn* in 1865 and *North Coast and Other Poems* in 1868, though he continued to write an occasional Scottish poem until the end of his career.

Unlike Burns, Buchanan uses in his Scottish poems a minimum of dialect—just a touch here and there to add savor. These poems, therefore, are easy for the non-Scot to comprehend. Certainly he had a non-Scottish audience in mind, for in his verse preface to the *Idylls* he bids the poems to "fly to the city" as a "spirit of the Spring" and to bring to the city dwellers pictures of Scottish life:

> Breathe softly on the eyes of those who read,
> And make a gentle picture of the scene
> Wherein these men and women come and go:
> The clachan with its humming sound of looms,
> The quaint old gables, roofs of turf and thatch,
> The glimmering spire that peeps above the firs,
> The stream whose soft blue arms encircle all,—
> And in the background heathery norland hills,
> Hued like the azure of the dew-berrie,
> And mingling with the regions of the rain![8]

Generally speaking, Buchanan adheres rather faithfully to this purpose throughout his Scottish poems—or at least he does so if we interpret the word *scene* as meaning the human scene, rather than pictures of nature. For, though some of the Scottish poems are devoted to scenes of natural beauty, most of them are primarily concerned with humans and their problems. Most of them, after the manner of Wordsworth, tell simple stories of simple peasant people.

The poems are divisible into two groups, the lyrics and the narratives; within these groups, they are additionally divisible into the inland poems and those of the seacoast. Thematically, they range even more variously to deal with such homely subjects as the struggle of a humble poet, the hopeless love of an idiot peasant for a heartless girl, the anguish of a dead mother for her children in the hands of a cruel stepmother, the grief of parents for their wayward daughter, the self-sacrifice of a fisher-boy, the fierce satire of a religious hypocrite.

While some of the Scottish poems are imitative of Burns and Wordsworth, others show considerable originality both in content and in treatment. The period of imitation was passing, and the young bard was discovering his own poetic voice. He sings confidently and effectively in "Poet Andrew" of the *Idylls* in telling the pathetic story of David Gray, a story which he was to tell later in prose in his *David Gray and Other Essays* of 1868. David's father, his voice broken with emotion, describes his son's last moments:

> . . . He smiled . . . and at the smile, I knew not why,
> It swam upon us, in a frosty pain,
> The end of a' was come at last, and Death
> Was creeping ben, his shadow on our hearts.
> We gazed on Andrew, call'd him by his name,
> And touch'd him softly . . . and he lay awhile,
> His een upon the snow, in a dark dream,
> Yet neither heard nor saw; but suddenly,
> He shook awa' the vision wi' a smile,
> Raised lustrous een, still smiling, to the sky,
> Next upon us, then dropt them to the flower
> That trembled in his hand, and murmur'd low,
> Like one that gladly murmurs to himsel'—
> 'Out of the Snow, the Snowdrop—out of Death
> Comes Life;' then closed his eyes and made a moan,
> And never spake another word again.[9]

An altogether different kind of Scottish lyric beauty pervades Buchanan's "The Song of the Shealing," celebrating the haunting quality of the song of the Scottish shepherdess:

> O who sits and sings the sad song of the Shealing,
>   Alone on the hill-side, alone in the night!
> Dead still through the shadows the moonlight is stealing,

> *The dew's on the heather, the mist on the height.*
> *She sitteth in silence, and singeth so slowly;*
> *She milks the dark kine with her fingers so fair,*
> *White woe of the lost, may her vigil be holy!*
> *The song of the shealing is sad on the air.*

And the final stanza:

> *O spirit of whiteness, O Ghost of the Shealing!*
> *Sing on, and sing low in the shade of the hill;*
> *The picture has faded your voice was revealing,*
> *The white owl looks out through the threshold so chill.*
> *There's a star on Ben Rannoch shines softly above you,*
> *It sparkles all night on the dew in your hair:*
> *White Soul of the Silence, we hear you and love you,—*
> *The song of the Shealing is sad on the air.* [10]

The note sounded throughout this poem is neither of Wordsworth
nor of Burns. The melancholy beauty of the scene blended with
the plaintive music reminds us more of Keats than of anybody
else, but it is Keats with a difference: a Scottish poet is singing a
Scottish song with something of the technique and craftsmanship
he had learned from Keats.

III   Poems of Protest

While the Owenite tradition that was strong in Buchanan impelled
him to protest against social evils wherever he saw them, he did
not preach Owenism or any other form of socialism as the panacea.
Instead, he seemed to recognize that social problems were far
too complex and deep-seated for any human power to cope with.
To the end of his life Buchanan continued to point to the many facets
of social injustice in the rapidly changing scene, but he always
concluded with the wistful hope that God, if indeed there was a
God, would appear and set things right. And, of course, as far as
Buchanan could see, God never did appear, and human affairs
grew more depressing with each passing year. The inevitable
consequence was that Buchanan became more despondent as life
went by, and he ended in pessimistic gloom even before the final
physical catastrophe fell upon him in 1900.

Social protest, therefore, is one of the dominant strains in
Buchanan's verse and can often be found lurking in the intonations
and implications of poems whose main purpose is concern with

disparate themes. But three books of poetry, each coming from a different period and inspired by a different body of experience, are sharply focused upon the evils of mankind as they impressed themselves upon Robert Buchanan. The first of these was the *London Poems* of 1866, his reaction to the widespread squalor and misery he saw in his first years in the metropolis. The second was *The Drama of Kings* of 1872, an angry outburst at the tyranny of kings, the brutality of war, and what Buchanan regarded as the cynical meddling of the Roman Catholic church. Third and last was his valedictory, or perhaps it should be called his maledictory, *The New Rome* of 1899, in which he accused Britain of being guilty of all the evils of pagan Rome.

In the *London Poems* Buchanan may well have had in mind such previous treatments of the London theme as Hogarth's sketches, Blake's London poems, and the novels of Fielding and Dickens. Certainly he emphasizes some of the same ideas. The sad plight of the fallen woman is the dominant theme in five of the most lengthy poems; the heartlessness of the great, impersonal city to those in desperate need recurs frequently. A spate of genre poems deals with various odds and ends of people about town, people not unlike many of those who fascinated Dickens and whom he made fascinating to the world: a dainty little milliner who goes about the city fearlessly; a profane old tailor and his equally profane parrot; a benevolent blind man who strolls every morning in company with a little girl who is mute; a "people's poet" who is ruined by the evils of patronage; a cruel and hypocritical attorney along the lines of Uriah Heap; an odd idealist who starves himself so that he may enjoy idle luxuries and may send money to the causes of Polish and Italian liberty; a professional hangman who sees only the evil in his fellow men; and a futile actress, Kitty Kemble, who spent her life pursuing fame, only to see it vanish in her embittered old age.

Three poems contain Buchanan's personal reflections about the city and about his 1866 book. In "Bexhill, 1866," he prefaces the poems by explaining that, although he had tried to write these verses in the city, he could not; he had had to go to the rural atmosphere of this suburb of London in order to sing. Still depressed by thoughts of the wretchedness of the distant metropolis, he explains that, if he tends to sing in melancholy strains, the reason lies in his sad reflections about London, all the more poignant

because of his grief for David Gray and for his father, lately dead
there. In "London, 1864," placed anachronously toward the end
of the volume, he complains that his growth in poetic power is
matched by a lessening of his élan for the profession of literature,
especially since it confines him to London. Much rather would he
be lying out in the mountains, surrounded by the inspiriting beauties
of nature; however, he philosophizes, even in the city his joy in
practicing his art more than counterbalances all other disadvantages.
The ecstasy of sending "his Soul up aloud" knows no equal.

He does not sing for maidens, schoolboys, or schoolmen, he
says in "L'Envoi" to the *London Poems*. He sings "for Dives and
the Devil too" and wishes that his song might rise to Heaven and
plumb the depths of Hell. Then he adds that, while some may pray
to God, "Lucifer's shall be the harvest song."[11] He wisely refrained
from explaining his precise meaning in this poem, but in *The
Devil's Case* of 1896 he makes it quite clear that he regards God
as a myth that must ultimately vanish from the serious consideration
of men; Satan, on the other hand, represents man's reliance upon
his own intellect. In the long run, man's intellectual progress,
Buchanan believes, will enable man to achieve utopia on earth.

Of the entire volume, the two poems attracting most attention
in 1866 were "Liz" and "Nell," two of the five pieces dealing with
the fallen woman. In 1866, the English were not quite ready to
face the problem; but they were aware of it. The early Victorian
view of the prostitute as a wicked woman was gradually giving
away to the concept that she was at least partially an unfortunate
victim of social and economic maladjustments. Dickens had skirted
the periphery of the problem in several of his novels of social protest.
In "Liz" and "Nell," Buchanan presents sexual irregularity as an
almost inevitable outgrowth of London slum life, as George
Bernard Shaw was to do later in his play, *Mrs. Warren's Profession*.
Liz, aged nineteen, is dying after giving birth to her illegitimate
child, a boy. She recounts the story of her life to a clergyman who
has been brought to her dingy room. Born in the slums and left an
orphan at an early age, she sold fruit in the streets to earn her living.
As she grew older, she saw other girls pairing off and living with
men as an accepted way of life, always without marriage. Then
she met Joe Purvis, like herself a child of the slums. They fell in
love and agreed to live together. The birth of their child has brought
her to her deathbed, unbeknown to Joe, who has presumably

been roaming the streets in the rain looking for work. As the poem closes, she hears Joe's footstep on the stairs and begs the clergyman to break the grim news to him:

> *There's Joe! I hear his foot upon the stairs!—*
> *He must be wet, poor lad!*
> *He will be angry, like enough, to find*
>   *Another little life to clothe and keep.*
> *But show him baby, Parson—speak him kind—*
>   *And tell him Doctor thinks I'm going to sleep.*
> *A hard, hard life is his! He need be strong*
> *And rough, to earn his bread and get along.*
> *I think he will be sorry when I go,*
>   *And leave the little one and him behind.*
>   *I hope he'll see another to his mind.*
> *To keep him straight and tidy. Poor old Joe!*[12]

In "Nell" the situation is much the same: another slum girl has just borne her first child to her common-law husband, Ned. She too is dying, but not solely from childbirth; her heart is broken because Ned has just been executed for murder. She has lost her will to live, and this factor, together with the birth after her having roamed the streets day and night preceding Ned's execution, is causing her death. The baby had been dead for several days before birth—since the day, in fact, in which the police had come to their hovel in the early morning to arrest Ned. In this poem, Buchanan pleads two cases. In addition to Nell, our sympathies are aroused for Ned, the slum boy who, following the usual pattern, takes to alcohol, in a drunken frenzy commits murder, and is hanged. Of course the real culprit is not Ned, not Nan, not alcohol, but society because of its easy toleration of the conditions rendering such crimes inevitable.

Buchanan's Owenism shows plainly in both "Liz" and "Nell." He is indicting a system, not individuals, although the indictment is never expressed in so many words. The reader is left with the inescapable conclusion that both Liz and Nell are the victims of social injustices which they did not create, which they could not control, and from which they could not escape. In such novels as *Oliver Twist* and *Nicholas Nickleby* Dickens had prodded the British conscience wide awake. Buchanan did not intend it to relapse into torpor.

Both poems are steeped in Victorian sentimentality and are

strongly tinged with melodrama. The Victorian audience loved its melodrama; and Buchanan, as he later demonstrated in his plays, had a strong penchant for melodrama and could write it effectively. In both poems the melodrama heightens the pathos of the cases Buchanan was laying at the doorstep of the Victorian public.

With the outbreak of the Franco-Prussian War in 1870, Buchanan, who was then living at Oban, put aside other interests to turn his attention to the spectacle across the Channel. Inspired by fierce sentiments expressed in Victor Hugo's *L'Année terrible* and by its exultation over the fall of Hugo's old enemy, Napoleon III, Buchanan, who greatly admired Hugo and hated Napoleon III, rushed into print with *Napoleon Fallen*, a book-length poem in dramatic form, in which he exults over the fall of the tyrant and the discomfiture of Roman Catholicism, which Buchanan saw as Napoleon's secret abettor. Toward the end of 1871 Buchanan made *Napoleon Fallen* into Act II of a three-act drama of which Act I portrays climactic scenes from the career of Napoleon I, and Act III shows the blood-and-iron character of Bismarck and the newly formed German Empire. This poem, which is in the form of Greek drama, with choral interludes of philosophical comment upon the characters and the action, is entitled *The Drama of Kings*.

Because Buchanan's thoughts had already turned to the question of the existence of the deity, it was inevitable that his protest would be linked to theological speculation as to why such debacles can be. The *Drama* begins with a "Prelude before the Curtain," in which Lucifer announces to the universal audience that it is to see a "Choric trilogy of tragedies" with earth as the scene; the time, the present; and the actors, men. The Author is to remain Unknown for the present, but He is of course God. In Act I, subtitled "France against the Teuton," Napoleon I is represented as a traitor who, at the height of his power after the victory of Jena, has misled the French people into the dark ways of imperialistic conquest. His only dread is of the Titan, the people, who may discover their betrayal and slay him before he can accomplish his chief purpose, to perpetuate his line on the throne of France. The act ends with a choric interlude prophesying his downfall.

Act II shows Napoleon III after his defeat at Sedan, imprisoned in the château of Wilhelmanone in Cassel. Bitterly he complains that the French people, whom he had tried to win by bribes, have betrayed him. He regrets his former leniency to them and plots to regain his throne. The intervening chorus gloats over his defeat and foresees that all kings past and present will meet the same end. At the same time it exclaims in sorrow over the misery of the French people and hurls imprecations at the "Teuton butchers." A second choric interlude berates England for not aiding her fallen sister, but she is too busy counting gold and has no time for nobler enterprises.

Act III, "The Teuton against Paris," deals with the fall of the city and the formation of the German Empire and contrasting scenes of desolation. Iron-hearted Bismarck provides hubris with his sneer that the downfall of France was a consequence of her wantonness; now she must expiate the wrongs done Germany by Napoleon I. Time himself, who speaks the epilogue, marvels that man is so stupid as to repeat the age-old mistakes of power and greed which always lead to a tragic conclusion. Time, the patriarch, longs for the final curtain to the tedious Drama of Man.

Then follows an "epilude," as Buchanan terms it, with all the actors appearing before God, who is a sort of grand director. When He criticizes Bismarck for playing a role too much like that of the two Napoleons, the actor removes his mask and reveals that he is Lucifer, who has also acted the parts of Napoleons I and III since no one else in the company could be prevailed upon to take those despicable roles. At this juncture, Lucifer asks God to hear the chorus sing a final song written by "a poor actor on the scene," none other than Buchanan. This song is positivistic: the souls of all who died for liberty shall rise just as certainly as winter gives way to spring. Man shall one day build a beautiful city where all shall be peace, happiness, and plenty. And there Christ, or at least the spirit of Christ, shall be reborn and shall live forever. Somewhat forced is this conclusion because nowhere in the *Drama* has Buchanan been able to find any evidence of God's existence, let alone any sign of His concern for human beings or their affairs. Nor has man shown any trace of profiting from past blunders in order to fashion a better future.

To the end of the *Drama* Buchanan appended a prose note "On Mystic Realism," defending his use of the form of Greek drama to present great historical events and claiming that it was an innovation in modern literature, as indeed it was.[13] He did not acknowledge that he had borrowed at least the germ of the idea from Hugo's *La Légende des siècles*.[14] Some justification for Buchanan's lack of acknowledgment lies in the fact that Hugo does not use the precise form of the Greek drama, while Buchanan adheres closely to the Greek model.

Buchanan himself later disavowed much of his work. Only parts of it are reprinted in the *Complete Poetical Works* of 1901, and these are prefaced with this remark: "The 'Drama of Kings' was written under a false conception, which no one discarded sooner than the author; but portions of it are preserved in the present collection, because, although written during the same feverish and evanescent excitement, they are the distinct lyrical products of the author's mind, and perfectly complete in themselves."[15] Presumably, his "false conception" was his condemnation of Napoleon III; he later viewed Bismarck as the real villain.

The *New Rome* of 1898 was Buchanan's retort to the complacency, the self-praise, and the chauvinism that characterized Queen Victoria's Diamond Jubilee of 1897, celebrating her achievement of the longest reign in English history. As most Britons saw it, God was indeed in His heaven and all was very right with the Empire. A few ominous clouds hovered on the foreign horizon, and some thorny domestic problems plagued the national conscience; but Britain would muddle through as she always had. Buchanan shared none of this optimism. And, when his old friend and admirer, Herbert Spencer, suggested to him that he should write "a satire on the times" and "denounce the miserable hypocrisy of our religious world, with its pretended observances of Christian principles, side by side with the abominations which it habitually assists and countenances," he set about the task with determination.[16]

The book opens with a poem, "To David in Heaven. Thirty Years After," in which he begs his dead friend to send him strength, for he stands in the arena of life with the mob demanding that he be thrown to the lions, a reference to the public disfavor into which he had fallen. With the winter of age approaching and with no personal belief in God, his only hope lies in his dead friend. For Buchanan lives in the midst of another Rome, on whose throne is "Christ with the crown of Antichrist," whose "legions shriek around him," and whose "creatures deify him."[17]

Even more harsh is the discord he sounds in "A Song of Jubilee," in which he warns Queen Victoria that many of her subjects are "butchering knaves," waiting for their chance to murder and rob other peoples as their ancestors have done throughout English history. But the real criminals are not the soldiers and sailors, he says in "The Mercenaries": Tommy Atkins is as much a victim as those he slays and who in turn slay him; the guilty are those who order him into battle. And the ruling powers instigate an endless series of wars solely to perpetuate the British Union, he asserts in "The Union." The Union itself is an acceptable governmental device, he cries; but it should be a Union of love and justice, not a robber Union to despoil other peoples.

Other injustices of the times are dealt with more briefly. "The Wearing of the Green" castigates the Irishmen who deserted Parnell and caused his downfall; "Sisters of Midnight," "The Lost Women," and "Annie" plead once again the case of fallen women; "Bicycle Song" hails the new freedom given women by the vehicle; "The New Buddha" takes Schopenhauer to task for his pessimism, while "Nietzsche" scorns the apostle of force as "nature's gutter-snipe"; "The Widow: A War Song" protests against the Boer War; and "Seraphina Snowe" satirizes the current British susceptibility to spiritualism.

Many of these poems are cleverly done, but the tone is so angry and strident that few achieve the music of true poetry. As the reviewer for the *Academy* remarked: "There is a vast deal of undisciplined vigour in this book, but the verses have been thrown together with the utmost recklessness and no suggestion of revision. Many of the pieces are mere unrhymed journalism."[18]

IV Poems of Personal Comment

As Buchanan had done in his critical essays, he used his *New Rome* to express his views on a wide variety of people and affairs. Generally, his likes and dislikes followed the patterns of his philosophical tenets as set forth in the essays, with, here and there, a minor divagation, but with many additions of people who had attracted his attention in the eleven years that lie between *A Look Round Literature* and *The New Rome*. Still at variance with Carlyle, he attacked him sharply for his derogatory views about the Negro. He still admired Gladstone, though he regretted his treatment of Parnell. The Salvation Army won his warm support, as set forth in his poem "Hallelujah Jane." Turning his attention to Tennyson, he confessed that he could neither comprehend nor partake of that poet's religious faith, nor could he share his optimism about the

future of the empire; but his admiration of Tennyson's artistic
greatness had not diminished. On the occasion of Tennyson's
death in 1892, Buchanan paid him a poetic tribute, appropriately
using the meter and rhyme of "In Memoriam" to do it:

> *I loved thy pleachèd English lawn,*
> *Thy gracious girls, thy pastoral lyre,*
> *Nay, even thy Church and slender spire*
> *Pointing at Heaven so far withdrawn!*
>
> *And often have I prayed to be*
> *As calm, as much at peace with God,—*
> *Not moaning underneath His rod,*
> *But smiling at His feet, with thee.*
>
> *Wherefore accept these songs of mine,*
> *For I, being lesson'd long in grief,*
> *Believe despite my unbelief,*
> *Although my faith is far from thine!*[19]

Two poems honor Walt Whitman, for whom Buchanan's ad-
miration was unswerving. "Socrates in Camden" was written at
Indian Rock, near Philadelphia, while Buchanan was visiting
America and shortly after he had journeyed to Camden to greet
the Sage. Whitman resembles Socrates, says Buchanan, because
he too loves nature and man; but, like Socrates, he was condemned
by prudish Boston because he dared to sing frankly of the body.
Then follows a résumé of American men of letters of the day:
Emerson is condemned; and Oliver Wendell Holmes, William
Dean Howells, and Henry James sneered at as "man-milliners,"
effeminate weaklings, of literature. Thomas Bailey Aldrich and
Charles Warren Stoddard are lauded; but, of course, Whitman is
extolled above all, Buchanan prophesying, as we have noted,
that he would outlast them all.

"The Gift of Burns" in *The New Rome* pronounces an encomium
upon his great countryman because, says Buchanan, he refused to
fawn upon rank and power. He never knelt to kings, but would
melt into prayer at a maiden's touch. Through the heritage he left,
all Scotsmen are ennobled, because he was "Our Singer, who has
made the Scot/ The Freeman of the World!"[20] a pardonable expression under the circumstances, for Buchanan wrote this poem
for, and read it at, the annual Burns Birthday Dinner of the
Caledonian Club of Boston.

Heinrich Heine wins an appreciative smile from Buchanan in "The Gnome," also included in *The New Rome*. He was a pixie, says Buchanan, who was especially adept at satirizing kings, queens, the Pope, and other dignitaries for whom the Scotsman had no love. But for Émile Zola, Armando Valdes, Arthur Rimbaud, Henrik Ibsen, Guy de Maupassant, Gustave Flaubert, and Oscar Wilde he has strong words of condemnation. In "The Dismal Throng" he holds them up to scorn as Naturalistic pessimists who delight in portraying the evil side of life. Away with them, says the Scotsman; let us have again writers who are robust and merry.

For the Socialist George Bernard Shaw, he has a friendly welcome. Although Shaw's laugh is "scornful," it is "medicinal" and much needed in modern Britain, "where prosperous priests with whores and warriors feed"[21]—an obvious allusion to Shaw's play *Mrs. Warren's Profession*, banned in Britain in 1898 because of its frankness about prostitution. Equally obvious is his sympathy for Thomas Hardy in another poem in *The New Rome*, "The Sad Shepherd." Depicting Hardy as a shepherd carrying "a wounded Lamb that bleateth in the cold" to the safety of the fold, Buchanan blesses his "midnight cry" and deems it "holier than the song/ The summer uplands heard at dawn of day!"[22] Hardy's last two novels, *Tess of the D'Urbervilles* in 1891 and *Jude the Obscure* in 1895 had brought upon him the strongest censure from the shocked British press, and Buchanan's allusion could be to either or both of these novels, though the "wounded Lamb" is more appropriate to *Tess* than to *Jude*.

Buchanan's final comment is upon himself. In "L'Envoi" to *The New Rome*, which he placed at the end of the *Complete Poetical Works* as the final L'Envoi for all his poetry, he sings defiantly, "I end as I began." Despite the slings and arrows of the world, he has not changed the fundamental principles of his life. He still believes in a life beyond the grave, though he has long ago cast away all the creeds "like husks of garner'd grain...."[23] His tears still flow for the poor and the weak; his reverence for woman has never abated; he still wars against lust and wrong; nor will he knuckle under to any "brazen Lie," no matter how formidable, no matter what the consequences; all fame is hollow unless it is won through aiding mankind. From his earliest remembrance, he says, he was convinced that he was not born to die. That conviction is with him as strong as ever, now that he stands facing death.

and has hailed as heroes "the Monsters of the earth, from Fritz [Frederick the Great] downwards."[45] Even the Sage's death did not lessen Buchanan's animosity, his characteristic reaction in such cases. Carlyle's works would not last, he exclaimed in a review of Wylie's life of Carlyle in the *Contemporary* in May, 1881. As for J. A. Froude's biography, Buchanan rejoiced that Froude had unintentionally dethroned his master by exposing how he had neglected the wife who loved him in favor of pursuing his literary ambitions. Posterity, says Buchanan, will agree with him that all of Carlyle's books are not worth "one of Jane Welsh's secret tears."[46]

And how has Carlyle fared? Unquestionably he and his gospel of the hero fell from grace with the rise of Hitler and his Nietzschean Superman of the 1930's. Carlyle has not vanished yet, but recent college anthologies of English literature show fewer and fewer pages devoted to him, and the *Annual Bibliographies* of the Modern Language Association reveal very little scholarly interest in him. That he will ever regain his former high pinnacle is dubious.

In his essays and poems in the 1890's Buchanan continued to condemn British imperialism and its unjust wars. In a notable essay in the *Contemporary Review* in December, 1899, "The Voice of the Hooligan," he inveighed against the "Barrack-Room Ballads" of Rudyard Kipling in an impassioned diatribe. This man is a hooligan, Buchanan cries; and his crude poems have been popularized by the corrupt press, the handmaiden to hooliganism and imperialism. Some poets have been praised because they uttered nothing base, but Kipling has almost never written anything that was not base. Devoid of any real thought, he has found acceptance because he always manages to say what the mob is thinking. He will not last; his star will fall even more rapidly than it rose. What a national ignominy to have such base strains in the land of Chaucer, Shakespeare, Wordsworth, and Shelley!

What is today's verdict? Kipling and imperialism went out of style with the advent of World War II. Critics fault him today for having been so engrossed with the British soldier in India and so self-deluded with his philosophy of the "white man's burden" that he was unable to perceive or to comprehend the vast stirrings of unrest that animated the Hindu people. He is read today chiefly for his children's stories.

In 1891, Buchanan published his last book of essays, *The Coming*

CHAPTER 5

In Quest of God

B UCHANAN'S poems of religion are of such importance that
they demand a chapter of their own. He himself regarded
them as the enduring work of his life, as the very summit of his
literary effort. He considered himself as peculiarly fitted by birth,
education, and inclination to be the religious poet of his times; and
he believed his times ideally suited for the religious poetry he
proposed to write. Alfred Tennyson, Robert Browning, Matthew
Arnold, Arthur Hugh Clough, and many other lesser nineteenth-
century poets had written of religious questions from the stand-
point of those who had been born and reared within the pale of
Christianity. Buchanan's intention was to present the views of one
who had lived his entire life without the pale, who was an Ishmael,
an outcast.

For a variety of reasons, religion was a questionable choice of
subject for Buchanan. We have already pointed out that, because of
the associations of his early life, religious speculation had become
almost an obsession, an ever-present cloud upon his mental horizon.
Moreover, since he approached religion from the viewpoint of an
unbeliever, he needed to propound sound theological and philosophical grounds for his dissent, grounds which Buchanan did not
have because he was neither a theologian nor a philosopher. Finally,
because Buchanan depended upon his pen for a living, he could
ill-afford to incur the displeasure of his public. He must have known
that his religious verse would cause the strongest adverse public
reaction, for he had the example of his father's missionary activities
to emphasize the danger. But he did not turn to less hazardous
topics because he felt that he had a message of great importance
that the world needed to hear. True to his motto, he had to tell the
truth and shame the devil, no matter at what personal cost. Speak
out he did, therefore, in a long series of poems beginning with
The Book of Orm in 1870 and ending with *The New Rome* in 1899.

As might be expected, his religious thinking was not original.
His ideas can easily be traced to Owenism, Positivism, German
Higher and Lower Criticism, Goethe's *Faust*, and to various other

odds and ends of thought which circulated among Victorian skeptics.
Like his father and Robert Owen, he could not believe in God
because of all the human wretchedness he saw in the world. Surely
a kind, beneficent, and almighty Creator would have so ordered
things that man, His creature, would be almost perfectly happy
on earth. He had not done so; therefore, He must not exist. Most
of the causes of human unhappiness can and must be removed,
Buchanan believed; but they had to be removed by man himself, as
both Owen and Auguste Comte had insisted. As for the God-
myth, it had been the chief obstacle to man's intellectual progress;
it had been used through the ages by evil tyrants and priests to
keep man in slavery so as to further their own selfish interests.
And the same evil forces had created the myth of Satan to frighten
man away from the use of his reason; otherwise, man might long
ago have realized to the full the gigantic hoax perpetrated upon
him and might have risen in wrath to break his chains and to
progress toward an earthly utopia much more rapidly than he had.
However, like most Victorian skeptics, Buchanan would not permit
himself to be labeled an atheist.[1] Like Owen, he admitted that
there was a great Power, or Principle, or Mystery, or Light that
governed the universe by laws beyond man's comprehension; and
He was, in the language of Herbert Spencer, the Unknowable, the
Infinite.

Aside from Buchanan's system of belief on his intellectual side,
there was also an emotional, superstitious, mystical facet to him
that was constantly at war with his intellectual side as determinedly
as the goodness of Dr. Jekyll warred with the evil of Mr. Hyde.
From his childhood days in Glasgow, Buchanan had been haunted
with the fear that he and his father were two infidel outcasts who
were totally wrong and that the great claims of Christianity were
right. If so, what disposition would be made of the two of them
when they stood before God's judgment seat? In answer to this
question, Buchanan introduced into his religious poetry its most
dominant theme—that of the outcast. His thesis is that God must
forgive the sincere dissenter, or outcast, no matter how mistaken he
might have been in his beliefs and practices on earth. His reasoning
is that, if God wishes man to believe in Him, all He needs to do is
to reveal Himself, and belief would be immediate and lasting.
Consequently, throughout his religious verse Buchanan pleads with
God to show Himself or to vouchsafe Buchanan some sign of

His existence. Without such a sign, surely God would not eternally condemn unbelievers like the two Buchanans.

About the immortality of the soul, Buchanan is ambivalent. Again, he has never seen conclusive proof of a life after death, but he cannot reject it because he cannot bear to believe that his beloved dead are gone forever or that nothing awaits himself but final darkness. His intense yearning to be reunited with his loved ones overpowers his intellectual skepticism. Likewise, his emotional side interferes with his complete acceptance of the Owenite doctrine that Jesus was really an earlier-day Owenite, a good man who taught brotherly love and other sound humanitarian principles but was not divine; that His great error was in leading His followers to believe Him the Son of God; that in all probability He was the illegitimate result of a guilty love affair that His mother had with another man. Emotionally, few men ever longed more intensely to believe in the great principles of Christianity than did Buchanan. Temperamentally, every instinct of his being disposed him toward an acceptance of its doctrines, a confession of his errors, and entry into its fold, and the happy life of the sound Christian. Every instinct, that is, except his intellectual skepticism, combined with the negative influences of his parentage and upbringing. Those held him back and forced him to remain a wanderer in the wasteland.

All these are the ideas that inform his religious poetry. His fundamental uncertainty robbed him of the soundness of conviction and the sureness of touch so necessary to great artistic achievement. His poems of doubt and despair seldom rise above ground level, but his poems of hope, especially his outcast poems, are the pinnacle of his literary achievement.

I The Book of Orm

Published in 1870, *The Book of Orm* shows the impact upon Buchanan of his father's death. He reflects upon the fate of his father's soul and devotes considerable thought to the state of his own beliefs and to his final destiny. Throughout the book his mind ranges over a wide field of theological speculation. The full title is *The Book of Orm: A Prelude to the Epic*, indicating that he already had in mind his *City of Dream*, though he did not publish it until 1888, and that he meant the *Book of Orm* to stand in somewhat the same relationship to the *City of Dream* as Wordsworth's *Prelude*

did to *The Excursion*. The chief difference is that Wordsworth's
Prelude is a poetic autobiography tracing the development of
thought, while Buchanan's *Orm* confines itself to theological meditations. For the main title, Buchanan harks back to Orm, the Augustin-
ian monk of the thirteenth century, whose *Ormulum* is a paraphrase
of the gospels written in Middle English for the benefit of the
common people who could not read Latin. Buchanan, of course,
is Orm. He speaks of Orm as "the Celt"; and, since Buchanan
considered himself as descended from Celtic Highlanders, the
analogy is not wholly inappropriate.

The *Book of Orm* is divided into ten major parts. In Part I, Orm
speculates as to why God veils His face from man; and he can
find no more satisfactory answer than that God Himself says it is
not yet time to unveil Himself. In the beginning, however, He did
reveal Himself to nature, who now puts forth her beauties so that
man may know that God is. In Part II, an allegory based on the
death of Buchanan Senior, Orm meets an old pilgrim whom he
tries to convert to a belief in God's existence and mercy; but the
old man has seen too much of the evil of the world to be persuaded.
Everywhere is the shadow of death, he answers; and this sad fact
prevents his acceptance of any optimistic view of life. Then, falling
by the wayside, the old man dies while Orm wonders where his
spirit has gone and whether it is happy and free. The death scene
leaves Orm shaken and uneasy.

In Part III, Orm wishes that death could vanish from the earth,
whereupon he has a vision that his wish has come true and that
men do not die but simply vanish when their end comes. This
occasions great discontent: people cry for the "good old days" of
death when they had at least a grave to remind them of their loved
ones. Orm wakens reconciled to the fact of death and thanks God
for the revelation. In Part IV, Orm meditates that, although death
parts us from those we love, we are still separated from them even
in life since every soul is imprisoned in a body and can never be
wholly known to any other soul. In Part V, Orm strives to believe
in God, but he is deterred by the same obstacle that blocked the
old Pilgrim—the pain, injustice, and rampant evil he sees everywhere.
In despair, he falls to his knees and begs God to show His face to
his anguished eyes.

In Part VI, Orm gets his wish: he looks up one day, and there
in the sky is the beautiful face of God. The face vanishes at night

but reappears the next day. As in the instance of vanishing death, the appearance of the face causes such dread and frenzy among men that they pray for its withdrawal. It disappears as Orm wakens with a sigh of relief that it was only another dream. Part VII, a cycle of thirty-four sonnets, is entitled "Coruisken Sonnets" because he wrote most of them on his meditations on the shores of Loch Coruisk near Oban. In content they vary between descriptions of the beautiful natural scenery and meditations upon the deity. The meditations, largely of a pessimistic turn, recapitulate the complaints of the previous six parts of the *Book of Orm*.

In Part VIII, Orm wanders by the Lake of Coruisk vainly reading his Bible for answers to his questions. Satan appears to him as the Prince of Intellectuals, offering to instruct Orm and causing to appear before him the shades of Socrates, Plato, King David, and many others. When Orm asks if the Crucifixion is a fable, Satan replies cryptically that it is a fable if men and women, their thoughts, feelings, and all they see are fables. Satan then vanishes with a request that Orm pray for him and all other outcast spirits.

Thus, early in his career Buchanan strikes a dominant idea of his religious philosophy: that Satan is the biblical counterpart to the pagan Prometheus; that he represents man's intellectual powers and progress but has been stigmatized by priests and tyrants through the ages because they have realized that the only way to keep man in slavery was to forbid intellectuality; that, as the friend of man, he has been cast into Hell by God; but that he is intrinsically good and may one day be released and forgiven. Buchanan makes clear that he has two meanings for the word *God*. In Part VIII, He is the fierce God of the Old Testament or the Zeus-Jupiter of pagan mythology, harsh and unjust. In defying Him to aid mankind, Satan is a humanitarian hero who should be revered by man, not hated. The real God, as Buchanan makes clear in the proem to the *Orm*, is

> . . . *the primal Mystery and Light,*
> *The most Unfathomable, Infinite,*
> *The Higher Law, Impersonal, Supreme,*
> *The Life in Life, the Dream within the Dream,*
> *The Fountain which in silent melody*
> *Feeds the dumb waters of Eternity,*
> *The Source whence every god hath flown and flows,*
> *And whither each departs to find repose.* [2]

And this source of all things has, of course, been served by Satan,
Plato, Socrates, Galileo, and all others who have aided man's
intellectual progress, including Buchanan's father and Buchanan
himself. In serving the real God, all of them have had to defy
the conventional God and the forces of tyranny and superstition
that enabled Him to keep man in intellectual slavery.

In Part IX, "The Devil's Mystics," Buchanan further develops
the idea that the mythical God is the villain and Satan the hero
of the story of creation. All the songs in this part, says Buchanan in
a poetic foreword, were in a manuscript which was washed to Orm's
feet as he stood on the shore of the sea. The implication, of course,
is that these poems are to be ascribed to Satan, not to Orm, and,
most certainly, not to Buchanan. Naturally, these poems would be
considered blasphemous by religious people; for the worst of them
is a savage parody on the Lord's Prayer, called here "The Devil's
Prayer".

> *Father, which art in Heaven,—not here below;*
>   *Be Thy name hallowëd, in that place of worth;*
> *The Waters of Life leapt, gleaming, gladdening):*
>   *Be Thy will done more tenderly on Earth;*
> *Since we must live—give us this day our bread;*
>   *Forgive our stumblings—since Thou mad'st us blind;*
> *If we offend Thee, Sire, at least forgive*
>   *As tenderly as we forgive our kind;—*
> *Spare us temptation,—human or divine;*
>   *Deliver us from evil, now and then;*
> *The Kingdom, Power, and Glory all are Thine*
>   *For ever and for evermore. Amen.* [3]

The *Book of Orm* closes with Part X, "The Vision of the Man
Accurst," which Harriett Jay says moved Buchanan to tears while
he was composing it. [4] As the title indicates, the theme is the outcast;
and it is Buchanan's first rendering of the idea and one of his best.
Its strength and beauty are far beyond anything else in the *Book of
Orm*. Of approximately three hundred lines, it is a poem that
deserves to live in the history of British verse. The setting is after
the Last Judgment, when all men have been redeemed except one
wretch who was so base that he had murdered his mother and had
deprived his wife of food and clothing. God casts him into outer
darkness, but his cries and curses so sorely disturb the blessed in
Heaven that God commands that he be questioned as to his wishes.

The man promises to go away and trouble Heaven no more with his cries if God will permit him to have just one soul to keep him company in his loneliness. When his wife and his mother volunteer to leave their heavenly homes and to share his wretchedness, their tender mercy breaks the man's iron defiance, and he weeps without restraint. The poem ends in a climax of compassion:

> And in a voice of most exceeding peace
> The Lord said (while against the Breast Divine
> The Waters of Life leapt, gleaming, gladdening) :
> "The Man is saved; let the Man enter in!"[5]

If Buchanan was aware that God as he shows Him here is very personal and anthropomorphic, not at all the "Impersonal, Supreme" he describes in the proem, he does not mention it. Obviously, his mood had changed from the intellectual to the emotional. For Buchanan, like most artists, was a creature of moods. He wanted not the "Impersonal, Supreme," but a warm, sympathetic God to appear personally and to assure Robert Buchanan of divine love and concern. Without such intimate and personal certification this doubting Thomas could not believe.

The *Book of Orm* encountered rough sailing in the reviews. The *Athenaeum* confessed that it could not understand much of the poem and disliked its rough meter.[6] The *London Quarterly* found it morbid and obscure.[7] The broadly tolerant *Westminster Review* objected to the bitterness of "The Devil's Mystics."[8] The *North British Review* thought the angry emotions exhibited in it were "unfit for poetic expression."[9] Never before had Buchanan encountered such unfavorable notices. The storm warnings were clearly up. If he persisted in his course, he could not doubt that even rougher seas awaited him.

II Balder the Beautiful

Buchanan did not publish his second book of religious poetry, *Balder the Beautiful*, until 1877. A product of his Irish residence from 1874 to 1877, *Balder* reflects a more tolerant view of religion with almost none of the frantic scolding and questioning of the *Book of Orm*. Quite possibly, his friendship in Ireland with the Catholic Father John Melvin and Father Michael Geraghty and with the Protestant minister, G. H. Croly, all of whom lived near

Buchanan and frequently associated with him, had something to do with his new-found tolerance. And, of course, the harsh reviews that greeted the *Book of Orm* might have persuaded him to temper his views so as to win a more favorable hearing.

Essentially, the views are not greatly changed from those of the *Book of Orm*, but they are considerably less offensive because they are set in Norse mythology rather than in the Judaic-Christian context. Buchanan still complains about the cruelty of God, but God is Odin, not Jehovah; and his Balder is as saddened and puzzled by the phenomenon of death as was Orm. Balder is so saddened, in fact, that he volunteers to go to his own death if his cruel father Odin will free man from death. Odin agrees to his son's proposal, then treacherously slays him, and Balder sinks into the arms of death. And there the deceitful King of the Gods leaves him, glad to be rid of a troublesome son whose life was a constant threat to his father's immortality. At this point Buchanan departs from the old myth to introduce Christ, who comes walking over the seas, clad in a winding sheet and bearing the stigmata on His hands and feet. He calls upon the dead Balder to rise, and he does. In reply to Balder's question as to His identity, Christ says He is Balder's "elder brother," that He also died for man, that those who love men most shall live and conquer death, but "the base shall die."

The spirit of death then asks Balder to take him to the abode of the gods, and the three set out. Arrived there, they encounter Odin, who asks Balder who the third figure is. When he learns it is Christ, Odin, shrieks in dismay that the old prophecy is realized, that he and the other gods must now die, for Balder has slain them. Balder is overcome with grief at the passing of his father and brothers, but Christ comforts him by saying that, if any of them were beautiful in spirit they shall live again; the base shall stay dead. The poem closes with heavenly choruses surrounding Balder and Christ and singing the theme song of the poem: "All that is beautiful shall abide,/All that is base shall die!"[10]

Buchanan prefaced his poem with a prose note admitting that his Odin had an "affinity" with Zeus and Jehovah, but he did not explain the precise nature of the relationship. He closed with a sly observation: "It is unnecessary, however, further to explain the spirit of a poem which each competent reader will interpret in his own way, and which, if it fulfils its purpose at all, should have many meanings for many minds."

Buchanan had high hopes for *Balder*. As he wrote to his friend William Canton: "For my own part, I am conceited enough to think it in some respects the finest conception of this generation!!!"[12] His extravagant claims met, however, with disappointment; for the busy world of 1877 did not share his excitement about the melding of Christianity with Norse mythology. Most of the reviewers confessed themselves puzzled by the obscure mysticism of the *Balder*, but they were ready to admit that it had some touches of good poetry. The *Illustrated News* found it too prosy and sermonic to be ranked as good poetry,[13] while the *Academy* observed dourly that it was only an ambitious failure.[14]

III *The "Ballad of Judas Iscariot"*

In 1874 Buchanan published his *Poetical Works of Robert Buchanan* in three volumes, the first of three collections of his poetry, the others occurring in 1884 and 1901. Included among them was the "Ballad of Judas Iscariot," not hitherto published in any of his books of verse. This poem is an impassioned restatement of the outcast theme of the "Vision of the Man Accurst," the concluding poem of the *Orm*. The soul of Judas, the betrayer of Christ, roams the world in a vain attempt to bury his dead body where no man may find it; but even the waters of a stagnant pool reject it. At last he comes to a lighted hall where Christ, the Bride-groom, sits waiting to pour the wine for the Lord's Supper. When he learns who moans without, Christ goes to the door to bid him welcome, despite the urgings of the other guests that He should scourge the soul of Judas away into the night. But Christ waves his hands, the air is filled with snowflakes which turn into doves who bear away the body of Judas. Jesus then beckons Judas's soul to enter, saying that He has delayed pouring the wine until the wandering sufferer's arrival. The poem ends with Judas entering; falling to his knees; and, after the fashion of Mary Magdalen, washing the Saviour's feet and drying them with his hair.

The story is effectively told in forty-nine stanzas in ballad form with an economy of words and with emotional restraint. The meter has a slow, plodding beat entirely suitable to the "Wandering Jew" motif, combined here with the "basest man" theme. Until the glory of the ending, the heavy pace of the poem reflects the utter weariness of a lost soul:

> *For days and nights he wandered on*
> *Upon an open plain,*
> *And the days went by like blinding mist,*
> *And the nights like rushing rain.*

> *For days and nights he wandered on,*
> *All thro' the Wood of Woe;*
> *And the nights went by like moaning wind,*
> *And the days like drifting snow.*[15]

But, when Jesus forgives him, the poem rises to the sublime of peace and joy:

> *'Twas the Bridegroom stood at the open door,*
> *And beckon'd, smiling sweet;*
> *'Twas the soul of Judas Iscariot*
> *Stole in, and fell at his feet.*

> *"The Holy Supper is spread within,*
> *And the many candles shine,*
> *And I have waited long for thee*
> *Before I poured the wine!*[16]

Once again, of course, the picture of God, or of Christ, in this instance, is anything but an "Impersonal, Supreme." He is as personal and as Christlike as any Christian could want Him. Since He is Christ, it would have been ridiculous to present Him as impersonal; and, since He is portrayed lovingly and reverently, Buchanan had no need of a previously prepared position to which he might retreat.

Altogether, the "Judas Iscariot" is one of Buchanan's best poems, as even so noted a critic as Lafcadio Hearn acclaims it. Whether or not it deserves Hearn's encomium as a poem "that will probably live as long as the English language . . . ."[17] is debatable. Up to now, it must be admitted, the decision leans toward the negative.

IV   The Earthquake

In November, 1885, following Buchanan's return to England from his American visit, he published *The Earthquake; or, Six Days and a Sabbath*. In a brief preface he announced that the second volume, containing the final three days and the Sabbath, was ready and would shortly come forth; but it never appeared, possibly because the poor reception given the first volume persuaded him to give it up as a wasted effort. The chief fault the reviewers found with *The Earthquake* was that it was such a close and un-inspired imitation of Boccaccio's *Decameron* that it constituted a plagiarism. And indeed the two works show so many similarities that the charge is irrefutable.

In the poem, earthquake shocks in contemporary London drive all from the city who can get away. The wealthy Lady Barbara of Kensington, spouse of an American millionaire, withdraws to her estate, the site of a former priory on the Tweed River, to which she invites her friends, authors, poets, scientists, the wealthy and famous, to share her sanctuary. To while away the time, they elect Barbara as Queen and set up a mock court, for which Barbara chooses her maids, cavaliers, a court fool (Douglas Sutherland of the *Cynical Review*), and Buchanan as her Laureate. The prime business of the court is to discuss, tell stories about, and speculate upon the great problems of life, death, and immortality—each day they are to treat a different aspect of the central theme. All agree that the Court should convene in the early afternoon of each day and sit until evening, after which all could be left to their own devices till the next day.

Within this framework, Buchanan has his characters express his views on such contemporary problems as the threat posed by Roman Catholicism, the divinity or nondivinity of Christ, the personality or impersonality of God, the rapid decrease of religious faith in England, the growing licentiousness of the times, the validity of pantheism, and the irreconciliations between religion and science. The book closes rather illogically with a poetic "Interlude," a fervid testimonial by Buchanan to the aid and inspiration his verses have been given by Harriett Jay. In a second interlude he states his determination to "sing of God on the mountain tops" and to attack injustice, hypocrisy, and oppression wherever he finds them.

We wonder why Buchanan wrote this poem. He obviously intended it to reflect the shifting intellectual currents of the times together with a portrayal of the personalities of such leading contemporary figures as Carlyle, Walt Whitman, George Eliot, and Walter Pater; but, as the poem moves along, these figures fade into the background along with Lady Barbara's court. Crowding into the foreground are Buchanan's own religious thoughts and reflections, inconclusive as always, and ending with the same yearning for a sign of God's existence that we saw in the *Book of Orm.*

He himself must have soon realized the absurdity of his basic structure in this poem in having a group of English intellectuals and dilettantes spend seven days debating with one another about such an anachronous subject as the immortality of the soul and the nature of God. He wisely dropped writing the second volume and brought his poem to a close at the end of the third day.

V   The City of Dream

A contributing cause to his abandonment of the *Earthquake* in midstream may well have been that it was superseded in his interest by *The City of Dream,* the epic of his religious wanderings, implied in the title of the *Book of Orm,* mentioned in the advertisements to the 1870 edition of *Napoleon Fallen,* and now (1888) nearing completion. This poem was to be his *magnum opus,* the supreme work climaxing his poetic career, the work which would boldly and frankly deal with the religious currents and cross-currents of the Victorian scene in an attempt to find that elusive haven of peace and faith that he had been actively seeking since the death of his father in 1866.

The basic idea of the poem was, of course, borrowed from Bunyan's *Pilgrim's Progress.* And, just as that work had been the allegory of Bunyan's religious wanderings, Buchanan's was to deal with his long search for God in the bewildering maze of Victorian theological speculation. The *Dream* was to be, in effect, an updating of Bunyan's work to the year 1888; it was to provide a similar highroad to faith for those who were bogged down in the shallows and miseries of religious uncertainty and perplexity. But, as Buchanan makes clear in his dedicatory poem, "To the Sainted Spirit of John Bunyan," with which he prefaces the *Dream,* this work was to be something quite different from Bunyan's "Fairy Tale Divine." For the day of Bunyan's dream was gone like the simple faith that had inspired it, and the God of whom Bunyan sang had fallen from His throne "like a meteor stone." Still, adds Buchanan, a spirit of truth resides in all creeds, no matter how obsolete. Therefore, the men of this later day, following "colder creeds" and seeking a much different kind of dream city as the goal of all their doubts and questions, could at least find "the higher truth of poesy divine" in Bunyan's work.

The dedication is consistent with a prose note at the end of the poem in which Buchanan states his purpose. This poem is meant to be "an epic of modern Revolt and Reconciliation" after the manner of such epics as Homer's *Odyssey*, Dante's *Divine Comedy*, Milton's *Paradise Lost*, and Bunyan's *Pilgrim's Progress*, which embodied the outstanding thought and inspiration of their days. And this book, Buchanan adds somewhat hopefully, aspires to be for the modern spirit of theological inquiry what the Puritan preacher's was and is for literal believers in dogmatic Christianity. His qualification for such a task is stated obliquely: "he [the reader] may never have realised to the full, as I have done, the existence of the City without God, or have come at last, footsore and despairing, to find solace and certainty on the brink of the Celestial Ocean."[18]

Before Buchanan arrives at his final vision, his soul has indeed had a harrowing experience. In a blank-verse poem of fifteen books and more than seventy-five hundred lines, he tells the story of his religious wanderings from childhood to the present. Significantly, he calls himself Ishmael, leaving no doubt that he regarded himself as a religious outcast. Following Bunyan's pattern, he presents the poem as a dream which he had had "in the noontide of my days,"[19] but the similarities to Buchanan's life are so numerous that we cannot doubt that he is poetically rendering in most instances what were actual experiences rather than an idealized vision. He flees from a dark city beside the sea, symbolizing the atheism of his early life, and travels inland because he has heard that up in the hills exists a beautiful city, the City of Dream, where all is peace and perfect bliss. An Evangelist, perhaps one of his early teachers, gives him a Bible, but Buchanan is repelled by the bloody tales of strife and terror. Next he encounters Hurricane, a grim Calvinist, whose fire-and-brimstone threats only depress him further. At this juncture Iconoclast, probably Buchanan's father, urges him to place no credence in the Bible, but to cast it over his shoulder. Buchanan admits that he now sees all the absurdities and contradictions of the Bible; but, when he asks Iconoclast in what he shall now put his faith, he receives no better advice than to return home, to work, and to forget his dream because there is no city beautiful.

But Ishmael-Buchanan, determined to push higher into the mountains ahead, wrings from Iconoclast the grudging admission that up in the hills lies the famed city of Christopolis, or Christianity.

Iconoclast confesses that he was born in this city but departed from it because it restricted his freedom. Warning Buchanan, or Ishmael, that he will not find it the city of which he dreams, Iconoclast leaves him.

Ishmael weighs Iconoclast's advice, but, inspired by his dream, proceeds upward; as he walks along, he reads in his Bible the story of Christ. He is enchanted until he comes to the agony of Gethsemane, where Christ cries, "O God, My God, if it may be,/Have mercy on Me, do not shed My blood!" Appalled by the horror of the Crucifixion, Ishmael asks, "How should this God have mercy upon men,/Seeing he spared not His anointed Son?"[20] These doubts are augmented by many encounters with skeptics who warn Ishmael that, when he arrives at Christopolis, he will not find it the city he anticipates. Christ is dead, they warn him; and His religion has fallen into the hands of charlatans and hypocrites. Shaken but not wholly deterred, he pushes on.

When he finally enters the gates of the city, he learns that the charges are only too true. The city is divided into two parts by a great wall: one half is Catholic; the other Protestant. Entering first into the Catholic half, Ishmael learns with dismay that it is dominated by hypocritical kings and conquerors who live in luxury and are oblivious to the hordes of beggars who live in the shadowy corners. The ruler of the city is a wrinkled old man carried in a splendid litter by priests, who cry, "Holy, holy." Anyone who questions the Pope's authority is immediately condemned by the priests and is fortunate if he escapes destruction. Ishmael's bold questions and even bolder objections to the teachings of Catholicism make him a marked man. He avoids disaster only by outracing the priests to the great brazen gate in the wall dividing the city and bearing the inscription, "Knock here if thou wouldst enter in." He knocks, the gate opens, and he is pulled to safety into the sanctuary of Protestantism. But here, too, much is to be desired. His rescuers are men in dark garments with sad faces, and this section of the city lacks the light and gaiety of the Catholic portion. With sinking heart he notes the same classes of kings and beggars that had disillusioned him with Catholicism; furthermore, he observes that all the gloomy ones hold open Bibles in their hands, reading as they walk slowly and sadly about.

Ishmael passionately cries that, though the Bible was originally meant for comfort, it had turned to wormwood long ago. In the dim light he discerns a troop of returning warriors who have been carrying on barbarous wars in the name of God, and he notes for the first 'time the dark chambers where silent men sit at tables counting heaps of gold which surround their open Bibles. Such capitalistic greed is too much for the Socialist in Ishmael, who cries out that Christ is indeed dead and that His religion has been completely distorted from His original teachings. Shouting that he will henceforth read only the Book of Nature, Ishmael draws his Bible from his bosom and casts it from him.

This sacrilege is too much for the grim Calvinists, who set upon him and beat him. Once more he escapes through a gate in the wall to which he is guided by a gentle priest named Merciful, who tries in vain to win him back to Christianity. Ishmael, who leaves him praying at the foot of a great crucifix, wends his way along a lonely road that leads upward from Christopolis. In succession, Ishmael tries and rejects atheism, paganism, Mohammedanism, and a sort of naturalism which worships "the Ever-changing yet Unchangeable" spirit of the universe. This spirit is "nameless and formless," not a personal god who builds cities, but a blind force which ever creates and destroys.[21] This spirit man can never know, says the hermit, Nightshade, who guides Ishmael at this stage of his journey. And when, for a fleeting second, the two see a specter flashing across the peaks and then dissolving into fiery vapor, Nightshade, possibly Buchanan's friend, Herbert Spencer, points to it and cries:

> *Behold*
> *The Spectre of the Inconceivable!*
> *The Light that flaming on the shuddering sense*
> *Within us fades, but flash'd from soul to soul*
> *Illumes that infinite ocean of sad thought*
> *We sail and sail for ever and find no shore!*
> *The Dream, the Dream! The Light that is the Life*
> *Within us and without us, yet eludes*
> *Our guessing—fades and changes, and is gone!"*[22]

But, because Ishmael's intense desire is to know God, he cannot be satisfied with such impersonality. He accordingly journeys on until he comes to the City without God, a Positivist metropolis far more beautiful than Christopolis. But here too the Pilgrim suffers disillusionment. From this city all the gods have been banished—even to call upon the name of God is forbidden—and science reigns unchallenged. This city is indeed an Owenite utopia

with libraries, gymnasiums, and a happy people who live in peace
and plenty. But Ishmael then discovers the birth hospitals wherein
are slaughtered all newborn babes who are blind, sick, or malformed.
Greatly disturbed, he enters a temple of medicine and prays that
the spirit of man may assume a visible form and appear to him;
but an aged virgin of the temple, who warns him not to blaspheme,
adds that the spirit of man is nameless and unknowable. If he must
pray, she states, he can pray to the statues of the great scientists
which stand about the temple. Disconsolately, he leaves this temple
only to enter another and to learn to his dismay that it is a temple
of vivisection. His anguish becomes intolerable when a dog about
to be butchered assumes the likeness of Christ. Ishmael, who calls
upon God to have mercy upon His Son, is immediately ejected
from the temple by the scientists.

A priest of the temple follows Ishmael outside to assure him that
God never existed and that Christ was only a madman whose
religion deluded mankind. But the scientists at work in the temple,
he assures his unwilling listener, "Have heal'd more wounds in
man's poor suffering flesh/Than e'er your Christ did open in man's
soul."[23] This very city, the Priest argues, proves the validity of
the Positivist doctrine because science has rid it of pestilence and
poverty, has made it a place of complete happiness. Not so, retorts
Ishmael, for death has not been vanquished here or anywhere. No,
but it has been modified, insists the Priest, for the old and weary
go willingly to the death chamber; they are comforted by scientific
knowledge that no force is ever lost and that their true immortality
lies in the children they leave behind them. Ishmael's retort is that
no one could be happy in this city, knowing that its very existence
was predicated upon the slaughter of deformed children and the
vivisection of innocent beasts.

Leaving the priest behind, Ishmael walks out of the city to the
crematorium where all the dead are disposed of. Here he engages
the old caretaker in conversation and learns that his suspicions are
well founded. When this city was Christian, the old man tells him,
people had disease, pain, and sorrow; but they died confidently,
even joyfully, for they had a hope of immortality. Now they die
gloomily and wearily because they see death as the end of every-
thing. Likewise, since both life and death are regarded as only
scientific phenomena, love and grief have nearly vanished from
human relationships.

Shuddering as a result of this recital, Ishmael looks beyond the crematorium and sees a vast land of shadows and forests. This primeval land is peopled with monsters and saurians, the old man tells him, though he has never been there himself. But Ishmael is so appalled by what he has heard and seen of the City without God, and is so anxious to leave this dreadful place that he runs to the edge of the precipice and leaps into the darkness—down into the forbidden land, losing consciousness as he falls.

Awakening, Ishmael finds that the old man has spoken truly. He is in a dismal land, "formless, chaotic, lonely, terrible"; it teems with serpents and saurian monsters, symbolizing, perhaps, the despair that seized Buchanan when the heartlessness of science forced him to abandon Positivism. He prays to God to deliver him from this dreadful place, and finally sees a steep path ascending into the mountains. Following it, he encounters an old man led by a beautiful female child. The old man, originally one of the builders of the City without God, tells Ishmael that the child led him from the city, through the dismal wasteland that Ishmael had traversed, and up this same path, seeking, but not yet finding, God. His acquaintance with the child has reassured him that God does exist, and he confidently awaits death so that he may see Him face to face.

When Ishmael demurs that he cannot share such optimism, the old man and the child take him to the heights, from which he looks out over a vast celestial ocean. They are now standing within God's temple, the old man tells him; if he but listens, he can hear the music of the spheres with God Himself as the veiled musician. Even as Ishmael murmurs that he had hoped to find an anthropomorphic God and a substantial heavenly city, he discerns on the shores of the celestial ocean the forms of an old man and a "maiden-like" woman, lying in their shrouds as though asleep. A heavenly choir sings, a boat with a hooded spirit in it approaches over the ocean, shadowy forms lift the two sleepers and place them in the boat as the choir chants a hymn of hope:

> *Forget me not, but come, O King,*
> *And find me softly slumbering*
> *In dark and troubled dreams of Thee—*
> *Then, with one waft of Thy bright wing,*
> *Awaken me!*[24]

Weeping, Ishmael-Buchanan watches the boat depart with what must be his father and his wife, his two beloved dead, aboard. The poem closes with a song in praise of death; for he now realizes, he says, that only through death may one enter the Celestial City of Dream and stand in the presence of the visible, living God.

Such is Buchanan's epic, the supreme effort of his poetic career upon which he staked his hope for lasting fame. The final scene is a statement of forlorn hope rather than belief. His dead fail to come to life within his vision, and God remains as much a mystery at the end of the quest as He had been at the beginning. The conclusion lacks the ringing exultation of the end of "The Man Accurst" and also the emotional fervor of "The Ballad of Judas Iscariot." It needed exactly such exuberant faith to bring it to an inspiring climax. Without it, Buchanan's protestation of his reconciliation to death has a hollow sound.

VI   The Outcast *Poems*

The publication of the *Dream* marks a turning point in Buchanan's career. The critical press greeted it with the same lack of favor with which it had received his earlier religious poetry. Typical of the journalistic attitude was the remark of the *Graphic* that this poem would not add to Buchanan's reputation: "It would . . . be grossly unfair to credit him with upholding the dreary, hopeless views put forward by Ishmael and others of his characters; but we fail to see what possible benefit to the world can accrue from their presentation in this form. Will any one be the wiser, better, or happier for such a book?"[25]

Harriett Jay says that he shrugged off his disappointment by reasoning that the British public wanted only "pretty verses" rather than real poetry;[26] but he had labored mightily with the *Dream*, and the bitterness aroused in him by its poor reception cast a shadow over his life from which he never fully emerged. Since he had bared his soul in the *Dream* and had revealed his intimate experiences, hopes, and fears, he could not help feeling humiliated by its rejection. In scorning his poem the world had scorned him also and had reaffirmed once more that he was an outcast. Significantly, from this time onward the outcast theme assumes ever greater prominence in his verse, reflecting the progressive darkening of his mind and spirit.

His chief religious poems after the *Dream* are *The Outcast* of 1891, *The Wandering Jew* of 1893, *The Devil's Case* of 1896, *The Ballad of Mary the Mother* in 1897, and "The Last Faith" of *The New Rome* in 1899. All are audacious attacks upon the major premises of orthodox religion, and they all re-sound the dominant theme of the outcast. Both *The Outcast* and *The Devil's Case* restate the Promethean idea of the *Book of Orm* that Satan's benevolent interest in man's political welfare and intellectual advancement has brought upon him the wrath of an unjust God. In *The Outcast*, he is Vanderdecken, the "Flying Dutchman" whose defiance of God has won him God's curse to sail the seas until he can find a woman who will love him so devotedly that she will voluntarily share his fate. In a South Sea island adventure, not a little indebted to Herman Melville's *Typee*, Vanderdecken finds such a girl; and, like Charles Maturin's Melmoth, from whom Buchanan has also borrowed liberally, Vanderdecken seems near the end of his quest. But the island maiden falls from a cliff and is killed; and, when Vanderdecken is given the option of having her brought back to life if he will give up his roving and live on the island with her, he chooses to let her remain dead and returns to his ship. Although he protests that his conscience prevents having her returned to the pain and anxiety of earthly existence, we are given to understand that his real reason is his love of the roving life.

The Devil's Case indulges in no such flights of Romantic whimsy. Walking one evening on Hampstead Heath, Buchanan encounters Satan seated on a fallen tree and reading the pink edition of the *Star*, a newspaper. The accounts of the evil and suffering published in the paper prove God's indifference to human misery, says the Devil, while he, the maligned one, has always been man's friend. Begging Buchanan to hear his case and report it accurately to mankind, Satan tells his story. It is the Promethean legend adapted so as to include material from Genesis, ancient and modern history, and the New Testament. Down through the ages Satan has fought a heroic and often discouraging fight; but now, in the nineteenth century, he believes that victory is at last in sight. False God-worship is rapidly diminishing before the advances of science, and the old plagues of war and poverty are evanescent.

When Buchanan, somewhat illogically, attempts to reassure Satan that God must have intended him to do the noble work that is nearing completion, and that his reward will be complete for-

giveness and a resumption of his original place in heaven, the
Devil is moved almost to tears. Then, stoutly maintaining that he
could not accept such salvation at the hands of One who has caused
so much suffering on earth, he leaves, charging Buchanan once more
to present his case to the world. The poem closes with "The Litany.
De Profundis," which, like "The Devil's Prayer" of the *Book of
Orm*, ironically begs God to save man from all the evils which He
has created and permits to exist on earth.

The Outcast and *The Devil's Case* strike a new note in Buchanan's
verse, for both are verse satires in the lightly mocking vein of
Byron's *Don Juan*. In *The Outcast*, for instance, Satan describes
his philosophical researches in racy rhymes that would not have
discredited Byron:

> *All this season,*
> *During my residence among you,*
> *I've search'd the poor stale scraps of reason*
> *The last Philosophers have flung you.*
> *I've read through Comte, the Catechism*
> *(Half common sense, half crank and schism),*
> *And Harriet Martineau's synopsis;*
> *Puzzled through Littré's monstr'-informous*
> *Encyclopaedia enormous,*
> *Until my brain grew blank as Topsy's;*
> *I've suck'd the bloodless books of Mill,*
> *As void of gall as any pigeon;*
> *I've swallow'd Congreve's patent pill*
> *To purge man's liver of Religion;*
> *I've tried my leisure to amuse*
> *With Freddy Harrison's reviews;*
> *I've thumb'd the essays of John Morley,*
> *So positive they made me poorly;*
> *Turning to follow with a smile*
> *The tea-cup tempests of Carlyle,*
> *I've been amazed at times to view*
> *The proselytes Tom fill'd with wonder—*
> *Ruskin, half seraph and half shrew,*
> *And divers dealers in cheap thunder.*
> *I've also, Heaven preserve me! read*
> *Daniel Deronda! which was worse*
> *Than any doom a wretch may dread,*
> *Except, of course, pragmatic verse!*[27]

As will have been noted, Buchanan also imitated Byron by taking occasional satirical flicks at other literary figures for whom he had little use. For, like Byron, he left little doubt of a strong connection between himself and his leading character. In fact, in both poems Satan reminds Buchanan that they have much in common: Buchanan is as much an outcast as he, says the Devil; for the poet dared in his epic to say that he cared for no gods, great or small.

The Wandering Jew is also an outcast poem, but from an altogether different angle. The tone is as elevated and as earnest as that of the *Dream* or "The Ballad of Judas Iscariot." The Wandering Jew is Jesus Himself, whom Buchanan meets as a cold, tired old man in the London streets on Christmas Eve. Buchanan swoons when he realizes who his companion is; when he revives, he finds himself outside the city on a plain at the foot of a mountain resembling Golgotha. Christ now bears His cross and is surrounded by vast multitudes who prick Him with spears and drive Him toward the mountain, where is seated a Judge who, though he seems human, has the body of a skeleton. Proclaiming himself to be the Spirit of Man, he stills the multitude and commands the people to leave Jesus to him.

As the trial proceeds, Jesus is accused by the multitude of perpetrating the lie that He has conquered death. The people denounce Him as a charlatan who, inspired by the example of John the Baptist, took to prophesying; his miracles were but tricks of magic and sleight-of-hand; but His greatest crime was rising from the tomb following His crucifixion, appearing to His apostles, and then never again showing Himself. A vast procession of witnesses are called to testify to Jesus's guilt; among them are Judas, Pilate, Marcus Aurelius, Buddha, Mohammed, Moses, Confucius, the Popes (whom He allowed to reign in vice), the great thinkers, scientists, and discoverers of all history.

When the Judge invites Jesus to present evidence in His defense, He replies that He is crushed with woe. He yearns to see His Father, from whom He has been absent since the moment of His birth; but, when He looks wearily to heaven, it is empty. The Judge promises to dismiss the case if Jesus will summon down His Father for all to see, but Jesus answers simply, "I bide my Father's time!"[28] Jesus weeps, but then rises in wrath and calls down endless woe upon a humanity that has never ceased to scorn Him and to sin in His name. The Judge, who commands Him to rise and take up

His cross, asks Him if He has anything more to say before sentence
is passed. He has: He begs that He be permitted to die. This request
the Judge refuses because He has slain men's acceptance of peaceful
death. He is therefore condemned to carry His cross and to wander
until the end of time searching for His Father. Thus the case is
resolved and adjudged—by Buchanan, of course, who is the real
judge. But he was still plagued by his old uncertainty, for the very
last line of *The Wandering Jew* is at once a prayer and a heartfelt
though paradoxical wish: "God help the Christ, that Christ may
help us all!"[29]

Significantly, *The Wandering Jew* is dedicated to Buchanan's
father: "To My Dear Father/Robert Buchanan/Poet and Social
Missionary/This Christmas Gift." And I believe the case against
Jesus here—as in the *Orm*, "Judas Iscariot," "The Vision of the
Man Accurst," the *Dream*, *The Outcast*, and *The Devil's Case*—
was meant, by implication, to be an exculpation of Buchanan's
father and Buchanan himself for their opposition to all organized
religions.

The theme of *The Ballad of Mary the Mother* is the sublimity of
mother-love, but here also is the strain of the outcast. In this case,
the outcast is Buchanan himself; he is cast out by other men because
he cannot accept Christ as the Son of God. The story of Jesus, as
Buchanan sees it, is what he presents in one of the most startling
and powerful of all his poems.

The story begins with Mary's begging those at the door of the
synagogue to tell Jesus, who is talking with His disciples inside,
that she and His brethren wish to speak with Him. But he refuses,
saying that His disciples are both mother and brethren to Him and
that no one else may enter. As she turns sorrowfully away, she
meets Mary Magdalene, who tells her that she loves Jesus so
passionately that she would rather be His "leman" than Caesar's
wife. But the mother tells the girl that her love is hopeless, for
Jesus is so fanatically bent upon what He conceives as His mission
that He will pay no more heed to the girl than He has to His mother.

Then follows the mother's pathetic tale, with the Magdalene as
the listener. As a maiden, the mother says, she had a liaison with a
man she refuses to name, and by him became pregnant with Jesus.
Keeping the secret to herself, she was panic-stricken when her
father betrothed and married her to the gentle Joseph. On their
wedding night she confessed her condition to her husband, who,

at first wrathful and on the point of casting her off, relented, forgave her, and accepted Jesus as his son. After Joseph's death, Jesus worked in the carpenter shop until the advent of John the Baptist, who so worked upon Jesus's imagination that He aspired to emulate him. He left the carpentry; went into the desert for a prolonged fast; and, when He returned, the mother perceived that He was a changed man. In the desert, He told His mother, He had seen the face of God in the heavens and, looking up, had heard God command Him to "go forth in thy Father's Name, For He hath chosen thee."[30]

From this time on, the mother has seen Him only fleetingly. She has heard rumors of His miracles, but on one occasion, when she saw him preaching to a multitude, he disappeared when the afflicted pressed Him to cure them. When the Magdalene interrupts to ask if the miracles were not performed, the mother sadly replies that no mortal hand could cure those afflicted by God; and Jesus is only mortal.

That night the mother hears Jesus, alone, praying to God to give Him the power to work miracles, but there is no reply. When He asks her if she believes in Him, or that He is the Son of God, she answers that Jesus is only mortal "and grew in thy mother's womb!"[31] Frowning, He turns away, saying: "Woe to thee, woman of little faith,/In the dawn of my Judgment Day!"[32]

At the Crucifixion, which she has known would be inevitable because of the rising anger of her people, Jesus turns His eyes not to Heaven, but down upon her as she stands at the foot of the cross and blesses her. Her Son finally returns to her when His dead body is taken down from the cross and she clasps His head to her breast. His sorrows are over, she murmurs; He, a mortal, sleeps in peace. He is not mortal, cries the Magdalene; and the poem ends with an altercation between two angry women.

In *The New Rome* of 1899, Buchanan grouped several poems on religious subjects under the general title "The Last Christians," indicating his belief that Christianity was obsolescent and would soon pass from the scene. One of these poems, "Storm in the Night," is addressed to Buchanan himself with the old refrain that Buchanan will never find Christ because Christ is dead. Another section of the book is devoted to a group of poems called "Latter-Day Gospels." One of these, "The Last Faith," reiterates Buchanan's faith in man's essential goodness. This faith is truly the last one a

man has; if he loses it, he loses all faith indeed. His own faith is
based on experience. He has haunted the streets at night to talk
with fallen women; he has been present at executions; he has
visited the most abject cases in hospitals. But always he has
discovered good, even in the most hardened and depraved.

The final poem of the "Gospels" is "Ad Carissimam Amicam,"
whom I believe to be his sister-in-law, Harriett Jay, who remained
with Buchanan after the death of his wife. As he looks abroad, he
sees the world rushing to doom; all the gods are dead; anarchy,
chaos, and night are settling down over all. But he can yet hope for
a new and better day to dawn, for its promise resides in the light
of love he sees in her eyes. Curiously enough, the ark of his religious
voyaging has finally come to rest on the same comforting firmament
of love that sustains Matthew Arnold in "Dover Beach." But
where Arnold's cry is a wail of despair, Buchanan's is a prayer of
faith:

> Deep in thy faithful eyes how bright the promise gleams,
> Answering the first faint beams of that new Dawn above—
> "Let there be LIGHT!" God said,—Light came in orient beams;
> Again across the Void, faint as a voice in dreams,
> God saith, "Let there be LOVE!"[33]

CHAPTER 6

The Writer of Plays

IF Buchanan had had his heart set on a career as a playwright, he could hardly have timed his arrival in London more opportunely than during 1860. For at that precise time the English theater, after more than sixty years in the doldrums, was emerging into one of its most productive, most stimulating epochs. Buchanan's role in this exciting development was a major one, for Allardyce Nicoll lists under his name the titles of fifty plays produced on the London stage over a period of thirty-seven years, beginning with *The Rathboys* in 1862 and concluding with *Two Little Maids from School* in 1898.[1]

Of these fifty plays, I have succeeded in obtaining the texts of forty-four from the Lord Chamberlain's Office in London and the Library of Congress in Washington. Sixteen of the forty-four are collaborations—seven of them with his sister-in-law, Harriett Jay, who also acted prominent roles in many of them. Of the twenty-eight remaining, eighteen are adaptations of the plays, novels, and—in the instances of Buchanan's *Marmion* and his *Pied Piper of Hamelin*—of the well-known dramatic poems of others. This leaves only ten plays which are, so far as I can determine, entirely Buchanan's own work. It is with these ten that I shall deal in this chapter, adding to them his *Sophia* and *Joseph's Sweetheart*, dramatizations of Henry Fielding's *Tom Jones* and *Joseph Andrews*, because Buchanan contributed to them so much of his own inspiration and genius that they deserve individual attention. For reasons I shall explain later, I shall include also one of his collaborative plays, *Alone in London*.

As Buchanan had done in his poetry, he soon showed that he was not content to be only a dramatist; he had to be a critic too. His criticisms, which cover a twenty-year span from 1876 to 1896,[2] are forceful and perceptive. They show clearly that Buchanan could have been a much greater playwright than he was, that he well knew how poor many of his theatrical offerings were, but that he was often forced by theater managers to write plays that were far beneath his own inclination and capability. They

121

explain somewhat the odd mixture of good and bad plays that
came from his pen: the poor ones were written in great haste and
at the request of theater managers; the good plays, which represent Buchanan's revolt against a highly restrictive and coercive
system, were written at the promptings and urgings of Buchanan's
intuitions and to satisfy his own integrity as an artist.

There is no mystery, then, as to why Buchanan was ashamed
of his role in the theater, nor why he stipulated to his collaborator,
G. R. Sims, that his name must not be used or published in any
way with his dramas.[3] While his collaborations with Sims brought
considerable money, Buchanan regarded them as trash and unworthy of the name which had been attached to *The City of Dream*
or to "The Ballad of Judas Iscariot."

But Buchanan did not suffer such shame without firing back
at the causes of it. His chief complaint against the Victorian theater
was directed at the hypocrisy and prudery of the Victorian audience
and against the reflection of these faults in the restrictions imposed
upon playwrights by the Lord Chamberlain's Office and by the
theater managers, who, he sneered, were dominated by the "British
Matron." These timid gentlemen he railed against because they
stifled experimentation in the drama. They refused to spend money
to mount any play which did not follow conventional patterns
and uphold conventional views, no matter how false and stupid
those patterns and views might be. The British people, Buchanan
contended, "would be a healthier race if their morals were less
tenderly taken care of," and "even morbid psychology is a healthier
thing than moral prudery or 'Podsnappery.' ... "[4] His personal
experience, he complained, had been that "whenever I have proposed any drama lofty in method or unconventional in form,
I have been met with the answer that such productions are inex-
pedient. Management is too precarious a business for experiments
of any kind."[5]

Buchanan's final remonstrance was against the noxious influence
of the drama critics in their attempts to coerce the drama into
the artificial directions of their preferences rather than permitting
it to follow freely the inclinations of the public. It was critical
meddling, he charged, which brought forth and forced upon the
public a plethora of problem plays after the fashion of Ibsen.
The result was that the public soon became surfeited with problem
plays and rejected them in favor of such inanities as variety shows,

musical pieces, and farcical comedies. Such trash now (1896) monopolized the theater, and "the hope of a rational drama, dealing with the great issues of modern life has been adjourned sine die. . . ."[6] But he stubbornly believed that good drama would rise again when the public taste demanded it. The lesson to be learned from this temporary setback, he insisted, was that "coterie journalism" must not be allowed to dictate to art.[7]

It is to be regretted that Buchanan did not take more seriously his theatrical career. His better plays present clear evidence of a real dramatic talent—a true sense of scene and character, an intuitive understanding of the capabilities of the theater—that could have made him one of the leading playwrights of the latter half of the nineteenth century. His tugging at the leash of the restrictions placed upon him by the Lord Chamberlain and by the theater managers, together with his frequent complaint of being forbidden to explore the problem areas of sex and marriage, suggests that he might have anticipated George Bernard Shaw in bringing such subjects to the stage. Shaw himself paid tribute to Buchanan's ability as a dramatist when he wrote in his review of Buchanan's and Miss Jay's *The Wanderer from Venus*, adapted from H. G. Well's novel, *The Wonderful Visit*, that "the play holds your attention and makes you believe in it: the born story-teller's imagination is in it unmistakeably. . . ." But Shaw also observed that Buchanan could have made it much better and could have endowed it with "distinction and felicity" if he had only given it some of the zeal he used "in writing letters to the papers, rehabilitating Satan, or committing literary assault and battery on somebody whose works he has not read."[8] As far as we know, Buchanan never retorted to Shaw's criticism; but if he had done so, it would have probably been something like this: "Why waste myself on an ephemeral theatrical toy which is subject to the whims of a Lord Chamberlain, a theater manager, and a fickle public? I consider it better and wiser to devote myself to my poetry and to the bar of the future."

Because of the haphazard conditions often surrounding the composition of Buchanan's plays, they do not follow the philosophical progression and development of his poems. Where they are adaptations of his own novels, they deal with some of his cherished causes and beliefs; otherwise, they concern themselves with topics of passing interest to the Victorian public. In the following discussion, I have arranged the plays in the order of their original production on the London stage, except for the last three, which have a common factor in that they deal with eighteenth-century materials. Such a classification has the merit of relating the plays to Buchanan's life, to his development as a playwright, and to the general history of the Victorian theater.

I *Learning the Trade*

Buchanan's first entirely original play, *The Witch Finder*, opened at Sadler's Wells on October 8, 1864.[9] Set in Salem, Massachusetts, during the witchcraft persecutions of 1692–94, this three-act melodrama revolves about Martin Holt, the witchcraft judge of the colony, who is revered by the Puritans for his apparent ability to detect witches. The plot reaches its climax when Holt judges that the evidence against an unknown person conclusively proves witchcraft, and then learns with consternation that the accused is his own daughter Ruth. The realization of what he has done drives him insane. But, just as Ruth is about to be burned at the stake, she is saved by the timely arrival of a ship from England with the word that the king has decreed all witchcraft trials null and void and has ordered such persecutions to cease at once. Her release restores her father to sanity, but he falls dead at the final curtain as Ruth finds solace in the arms of her lover, Walter Vane, one of the few men in the colony who had refused to subscribe to the witchcraft craze.

This extravagant melodrama seems almost farcical today. The dialogue and the characterizations are equally preposterous. However, audiences in 1864 were not so critical as they became even ten years later; and we have Harriett Jay's word that *The Witch Finder* "met with an excellent reception."[10] Nevertheless, the venture must not have been very profitable, for Buchanan allowed ten years to elapse before his next play, *The Madcap Prince*, an adaptation of Sir Walter Scott's novel *Woodstock* in 1874.

Buchanan's next original play, *Corinne*, opened at the Lyceum on June 26, 1876. A melodramatic tragedy in four acts, this play has the dual purpose of asserting the nobility of the acting profession and of condemning the tyranny of the Catholic church, which, in pre-Revolutionary France, had refused to allow an actress to be buried in consecrated ground. The play had a very short run. Buchanan blamed its failure upon the ineptitude of the actress who played the leading role, a Mrs. Fairfax, to whom Buchanan sold the play outright, and who produced it herself.[11] But the reviewer for the *Illustrated London News* judged that it bored the London audience because it dealt with a hackneyed subject—the French Revolution—and because it was poorly written.[12] A reading of the manuscript inclines me to agree with the reviewer, although it is equally evident that *Corinne* represents a considerable advance in dramatic skill and technique over *The Witch Finder*. In both plays Buchanan was of course indulging his Owenite and Positivistic leanings by attacking religion for its bigotry, its injustice, and its corruption.

Somewhat better fortune greeted his adaptation of his first novel, *The Shadow of the Sword*, which was produced under the same title at Brighton on May 9, 1881, and again at the Olympic in London on April 8, 1882. This play deals with the fierce hatred of war by a young French peasant, Rohan Gwenfern, and with his efforts to avoid conscription into the armies of Napoleon I. The play is, of course, extremely melodramatic. It is the sort of thing that Buchanan was ashamed of and that led him to resort to a pseudonym, but it represents the level of entertainment that the more poorly educated elements of the Victorian audience loved and would patronize.

G. R. Sims says that Buchanan often directed rehearsals of his plays, brandishing his umbrella and beating it on the prompter's table to emphasize declamatory passages.[13] In the manuscript of *The Shadow of the Sword* are many director's notes and stage drawings, indicating that Buchanan probably played an important role in the staging of his work. Such experiences are invaluable in educating a young playwright to the potentialities and limitations of the theater. Some of Buchanan's later plays show that he was an apt pupil.

Buchanan's first real success in the theater was scored with *Stormbeaten*, produced at the temple of Victorian melodrama, the Adelphi, on March 14, 1883. A dramatization in five acts of his novel *God and the Man* of 1881, the title change was necessitated by the refusal of the Lord Chancellor to license any play which used the name of the deity. The play is largely faithful to the novel, which, as Buchanan said in his preface to the edition of it in 1883, was intended as a study of the folly of human hatred. The novel, as we have seen, was also a vehicle for his own apology to Dante Gabriel Rossetti; but Buchanan had the good taste to omit the apology or any reference to it from the play. He did, however, make some unfortunate changes in the drama to make it even more melodramatic than the novel, the most notable being that, instead of having the villain die in the polar regions, he brings him back to England and to a life of wedded bliss with the girl he had seduced, Kate Christianson, the sister of the hero. This change was, of course, a concession to the well-known taste of the Adelphi audiences, who liked their plays to end in complete happiness. Buchanan obliged them, for his final curtain descends upon conditions of total love and forgiveness.

Stormbeaten was well cast, well acted, and favorably reviewed except by a few critics who held that Orchardson had been portrayed as too villainous a character for his final repentance to be convincing. The elaborate polar scene with icebergs and shipwreck afforded ample opportunity for the kind of spectacle that thrilled the Adelphi audience, while the acting of Beerbohm Tree, who played the role of a shepherd, introduced into the play to provide comic relief, attracted special mention. So successful was this drama that the *Illustrated London News* for May 5, 1883, devoted an entire page to pictures of its cast and scenery. It was later staged in New York, where it found less success.[14] However, Harriett Jay says the spectators showed their approval to such a degree that successive performances brought Buchanan more money than he had made from all his previous plays. Since *Stormbeaten* was his ninth play on the London stage, his financial harvest from it, according to Miss Jay's formula, must have been considerable.

II   *The Middle Years, 1885–1890*

While I have decided to exclude from this discussion all the plays in which Buchanan collaborated with others, I am making an exception of his *Alone in London*, in which he announced that his sister-in-law, Miss Harriett Jay, was his collaborator. My reasons for the exception are that it was far and away the most popular of all Buchanan's plays and that, since it was the very first instance of Miss Jay's collaborating with him, I believe that her part in the actual writing was quite minor and that the play was largely Buchanan's work. The entire play was written during the two to three weeks of a voyage to America in 1884, a voyage on which Buchanan was accompanied by Harriett Jay. Buchanan himself produced and probably also directed it at the Chestnut Street Theater in Philadelphia, later selling the American rights.[15] Returning to England a few months later, he had the play produced at the Olympic Theatre in the Strand, where it was immediately popular, earning him more money than he was to make from any single literary venture during his entire career. However, because it was another extreme melodrama, Buchanan was ashamed of *Alone in London*; and he sold it for a mere fraction of the huge sum it was to earn within the next ten years.[16]

Alone in London, a typical Victorian melodrama, centers about the basic story of an innocent girl who marries a villain and is persecuted by him until his welcome death at the final curtain. On this framework Buchanan hung not a few borrowings from the novels of Dickens, both in character and situation, including a Sidney Carton-like hero named John Biddlecomb, who remains faithful to the heroine in spite of her having married the villain; a scene from the *Old Curiosity Shop* in which the villain tries to drown the heroine by locking her in a sluicehouse and then opening the sluice gates to let in the river; a pathetic, malformed character named Chickweed, who owes much to Smike from *Nicholas Nickleby*; and a situation in which the heroine's son Paul is forced by the villain to aid him in breaking into a bank, a close imitation of one of the incidents in *Oliver Twist*. By progressive stages the villain is made so obnoxious that the audience thirsts for his blood, and the thirst is satisfied in the conclusion when the rascal is stabbed to death by Chickweed, whose deformity was caused by a terrible beating given him years before by the villain.

Buchanan's adaptation of his own novel, *The Child of Nature*, was given at the Novelty Theatre on November 12, 1887, as a five-act melodrama entitled *The Blue Bells of Scotland*. Although the plot of the play is considerably changed from that of the novel, the theme of social protest is preserved: the economic injustices heaped upon impoverished Highlanders by the harsh overseers of absentee English landlords. When an Englishwoman and a wealthy young Englishman fall in love with a poor but noble young Highlander and his sister, respectively, the young Englishman abducts and wrongs the Highland girl through the old trick of a fake marriage. But all comes right in the end when the young Englishman dies of wounds in India, after having acknowledged the young Scottish girl as his wife and leaving both his title and his fortune to the young Scot, who, it turns out, is his distant cousin. Other than the Scottish materials, *The Blue Bells* offers nothing worthy of note.

As its title indicates, *The Old Home*, given as a matinee at the Vaudeville on June 19, 1889, is a melodrama. But it is not pure melodrama; it is a curious hybrid of the sophisticated comedy of manners and the melodrama. A dissolute, titled London rake marries the daughter of a wealthy Australian sheep farmer for her money. After the marriage, he and his friends openly ridicule the wife and her untutored father, and the rake continues his philandering with a former flame. Discovering her husband's apparent seduction of an innocent girl, the wife leaves him in disgust; and she and her father prepare to return to Australia. But all is made right when the husband is proven innocent of the seduction. Realizing that he now truly loves his wife, he promises to reform his rakish ways; and the curtain falls on what can only be called a potboiler and one of the flimsiest of Buchanan's theatrical efforts. In all probability it was dashed off in great haste to raise some much needed money for an impecunious Scotsman.

Whether or not a wife should be legally bound to a husband who is totally unsuited to her, who treats her cruelly and even inhumanly, and who is a villain and a libertine is the central question of Buchanan's next play, a three-act drama in prose, *The Man and the Woman*, given as a matinee at the Criterion on December 19, 1889. At that date, English laws gave an affirmative answer to the question. In protest against those laws, Buchanan wrote this play, just as he had written his novel *The Martyrdom of Madeline* in 1882. The same question is raised in *Alone in London*, although not so stridently as in this play. The reason for Buchanan's greater frankness and daring is not difficult to find. Probably the underlying reason was that movement toward exploring the dark corners of social problems, especially those relating to sex and the real nature of woman, which was a definite sociological phenomenon of the 1880's and 1890's. The movement was helped along by an increasing realism in the discussion of social questions in the plays of Thomas William Robertson, Arthur Wing Pinero, and Henry Arthur Jones; and it burgeoned into full bloom with the translation into English and presentation on the London stage of the social dramas of Henrik Ibsen in the 1880's and 1890's. Indeed, a revolution in the English theater was quietly gaining headway, and it reached a climax in the 1890's with George Bernard Shaw's *Widower's Houses* and *Mrs. Warren's Profession.*

Every aspect of Buchanan's plot is devised to make the marriage laws completely absurd in insisting that a wife is still legally bound to a totally worthless and cruel husband. His villainous husband is an Irishman, Philip O'Mara, who had brutally mistreated his wife Gillian, had squandered all her money, and then, abandoning his wife and baby daughter, Dora, had run off to America. Years pass, and Gillian builds a new life for herself and Dora in a little village of Essex with the help of a kindly Anglican clergyman, Dr. Edgar Bream. When word comes from America that O'Mara has died there, Sir George Venables, a well-to-do landowner and baronet of the vicinity, who has long loved Gillian, asks her to be his wife. She consents, but insists that he hear the story of her life and marriage. He is not deterred, and marriage plans are proceeding rapidly when O'Mara appears (the report of his death had been entirely false) and tells her that he has returned because he has learned that she has inherited some money from her uncle. He insists that Gillian must take him back, for he is still her husband. To enforce his demands, he kidnaps the child, Dora, and refuses to return her. Distracted, Gillian says she will go to law to force him to return the child. She proclaims openly that she loves Sir George and has no affection at all for O'Mara. O'Mara sneers that, if she goes to court, he will humiliate both her and Sir George; he boasts that he is certain that English law will find him in the right.

At this point an interesting and significant argument takes place between the old Anglican pastor of the village, the Reverend Herbert, and his assistant, Dr. Bream, Gillian's friend. The Reverend Herbert insists that O'Mara is still Gillian's proper husband and that she must return to him. Dr. Bream holds that O'Mara has forfeited all claim upon Gillian and that she is entirely free of him. Sir George, of course, is decidedly of Bream's opinion. Just as O'Mara is about to make an exit, taking Dora with him and promising all kinds of exposure and embarrassment in court, there appears in the doorway the husband of a married woman whom O'Mara had seduced and whose death he had caused.

He stabs and kills O'Mara, thus solving the problem in precisely the same fashion as a similar problem had been solved in *Alone in London*.

Since Buchanan was one of the first English dramatists to follow Ibsen's lead, he must be credited with being a pioneer in breaking up the log-jam of Victorian prudery. After him, in the 1890's, came J. T. Grein and the Independent Theatre Society; the beginning of the problem plays of George Bernard Shaw; and the equally defiant novels of Thomas Hardy, *Tess of the D'Urbervilles* and *Jude the Obscure*. By the end of the century, the log-jam was well broken, and the literary and social currents were moving with increasing rapidity toward the frankness of the new age.

"Mr. Buchanan should dip again into Keats before he meddles with a theme such as this, and after so doing will probably leave it alone," said the *Athenaeum* of Buchanan's *The Bride of Love*, a four-act drama in blank verse presented on May 21, 1890.[17] If dramatized at all, said the reviewer, such a tale should have been translated into a comic opera in this latter day of sophistication. Oddly enough, the reviewer did not discuss the incongruity of presenting to the relatively uncultured Adelphi audience, strongly addicted as it was to extreme melodrama, this delicate poetic fantasy of how Psyche became immortal through her love of the god Eros.

Buchanan's intense but skeptical interest in spiritualism underlies his play *The Charlatan*, produced at the Haymarket on January 8, 1894.[18] The plot turns about two unscrupulous mesmerists and spiritualists who seek to use their powers and their tricks to prey upon others. One of these is Philip Woodville, a young man of mixed English and Hindu blood, who pursues the heroine, Isabel Arlington, to England in an attempt to force her to marry him. Because her mother is dead and her father has been lost on an expedition to Tibet, she goes to the country estate of her uncle, the Earl of Wanbrough. Unfortunately the Earl and his son, Isabel's cousin, Mervin Darrell, are already under the influence of an accomplice of Woodville, a Madame Obnoskin, also a spiritualist, as well as the originator and expounder of Theosophy. She is obviously Buchanan's derisive portrayal of the well-known Madame Helena Blavatsky, who figured prominently among English believers in the occult in the 1880's. Madame Obnoskin has matrimonial designs upon the Earl and is well along toward accomplishing them. With her assistance and without Isabel's knowledge, Woodville easily manages an invitation to the Earl's country estate.

The play reaches a climax when Woodville uses his mesmeric powers to draw the sleep-walking Isabel to his room in the dead of night; but, as he is about to ravish her, she, still under the spell, confesses that she loves him. The confession touches his better nature. He arouses her; proclaims his now-abandoned evil intentions; and, when members of the family knock at his door, saves her reputation by sending her back to her room by another exit. The next morning he makes a frank and complete confession to the Earl of his and Madame Obnoskin's spiritualist fakery—without divulging Isabel's visit to his room—and asks Isabel to forgive him for pursuing her to England. At this juncture Madame Obnoskin, smarting under Woodville's exposure of her and the consequent ruin of her plans to become Lady Wanbrough, reveals Isabel's visit to Woodville's room. While the Earl and the family stand aghast, Isabel proudly proclaims her love for Woodville and begs him to stay. He, however, is steadfast in his determination to leave for at least a year in order to prove himself worthy of her by his reformation. If he succeeds, he promises, he will return and claim her. And so the play ends.

While *The Charlatan* was not a smash hit, it did have considerable success. The plot was both original and, in view of the contemporary interest in spiritualism, timely. The dialogue was adequate. The cast, headed by Beerbohm Tree as Woodville and his wife as Isabel, was one of the best.

In *Lady Gladys*, a four-act melodrama produced at the Haymarket on May 7, 1894, we have once again Buchanan's favorite pattern of two inimical families with the son of one marrying the daughter of the other. In this case, the love is all on the side of the son, and the daughter marries him for revenge rather than love. However, she discovers her husband's true nobility of character; and, when he falls dangerously ill of the old Victorian malady of brain fever, her hatred turns into pity and then into love, so that the final curtain falls on a scene of forgiveness and happiness. The play met with scant success, possibly because the public appetite for melodrama had noticeably lessened.

III *In Praise of Fielding and Sheridan*

In the latter part of his theatrical career, Buchanan made three notable incursions into eighteenth-century materials: his *Sophia*, an adaptation of Sir Henry Fielding's novel *Tom Jones*; *Joseph's Sweetheart*, adapted from Fielding's *Joseph Andrews*; and *Dick Sheridan*, an original play based on the love story of Richard Sheridan and Elizabeth Linley. These three plays are easily among Buchanan's best. Although in each case the story lines had been firmly established by the original materials, Buchanan changed them at will; and most of his changes are cleverly conceived. The dialogue sparkles with a wit that is mostly Buchanan's, and the characters are skillfully drawn. In all three plays dramatic interest is created early, and it rises consistently until the final curtain.

I suspect that *Sophia* was intended as a trial balloon to test the Victorian temper on the important matter of sexual frankness. A clever adaptation of *Tom Jones*, shorn of its most objectionable materials but with much of its earthiness still present, it made an excellent test case to determine whether the old taboos were still in force, and to what degree. However, the test case did not easily get a hearing since *Sophia* made the rounds of the theater managers of London for ten years and was rejected by them as too expensive to stage and as too risqué for the Victorian public. When finally produced by Thomas Thorne at the Vaudeville Theatre on April 17, 1886, it went slowly at first, but then rose rapidly to such popularity that it ran consecutively for over five hundred nights and brought Buchanan rich returns, as well as the gratification of proving that he had been right and the theater managers wrong in the assessment of public opinion.

Buchanan carefully omits from his play such earthy portions of the novel as Tom's promiscuity and involvement with Molly Seagrim, Square's "natural" indulgence with Molly, the incidents involving Jennie Jones and Ensign Northerton, the adventures at the inn on the road to London, and the final revelation that Tom is the son of Squire Allworthy's sister. Indeed, the fact that Tom was a foundling is never mentioned; in the opening scenes Allworthy simply reminds Tom that he had been brought to Allworthy as a baby and that he had accepted him as a gift from Heaven. The affair with Lady Bellaston is reduced to the respectable level of her seeking to marry Tom because she is attracted to him, while

Lord Fellamar and his attempted rape of Sophia are omitted altogether. Blifil is made an even greater hypocrite than Fielding presents him by having him guilty of an amour with Molly and then blaming her ensuing pregnancy on Tom. Molly's father, Black George, has learned of the connection between Blifil and Molly; and, when Squire Western imprisons Black George for poaching, he threatens to expose Blifil unless he helps him escape from prison. Blifil manages the escape, but he fastens this blame also upon Tom, who is therefore banished by Allworthy.

A good example of Buchanan's clever original dialogue and of his suiting it to the characters of the novel is this scene from Act I in which Tom's too heavy drinking at a social gathering at the home of Squire Western and Sophia provokes a lively discussion:

SQ. WEST. . . . Tom for my money—eh neighbour Copse?

COPSE. Right, neighbour. Lord, to see him take a fence on the black filly! It be like an angel a-flying!

SQ. WEST. Or to hear him singing the last flash songs from Lunnon, or to see him a-playing kiss-in-the-ring wi' the gals on harvest-night!

SQUARE. These are coarse pleasures. My other pupil disdains the village herd. *Ubi profanum, vulgus,* he sings with Horace.

SQ. WESTERN. That for Horace; tho' he be a friend o' yourn I'd like to lend un a flick. (*Shouts.*) Tom! Tom! ye rogue, where are you?

(*Enter Miss Western—Sophia and Blifil.*)

MISS WEST. Prithee not so loud, brother. You are obstreperous.

SQ. WEST. Obstropelous yourself! I wasn't calling for *thee.*

ALLWORTHY. Nay, nay, my dear Western—

SQ. WEST. Then what does she call names for? I'm no more obstropelis than she is!

MISS WEST. I declare, brother, that your vulgarity is unbearable. Your person smells of the stable, and every word you utter is worthy of a groom. Prithee stand further off! You offend my olfactory organs!

SQ. WEST. That for your oil-factory organs! I'll smell as I please and shout as I please in my own garden. (*Crosses to table.*)

(*Tea is brought by* SERVANTS, *and* MISS WESTERN *presides at a table near glass doors. Company group themselves.*)

SOPHIA. Shall I fetch you a dish of tea, papa?

SQ. WEST. Not for I, not for I! Tea be for women volks, not for I. Tom! where are you? Tom Jones!

(*Imitates huntsman's cry, and runs out.*)

MISS WEST. (*Pouring tea*) I declare, gentlemen, that I deserve your commiseration. My brother is unbearable.

ALLWORTHY. (*Sipping from cup.*) The roughness of his country manners is nothing—it is balanced by the goodness of his heart.

MISS WEST. Thank Heaven I was not brought up in the country, if those be country manners. Mr. Blifil, shall I give you another cup?

BLIFIL. Thank you, madam. (*Affectedly*) This tea has a delicious fragrance!

SQUARE. Positively, ambrosia! How much to be commended above those fermented liquors which steal the wits away and turn man into a swine!

MISS W. *You* don't drink wine, dear Mr. Blifil.

BLI. I have been taught by my honoured preceptor to imbibe no fluid of any intoxicating nature.

MISS W. Sophia!

SOPH. (*Carelessly*) Yes, Aunt.

MISS W. Listen to Mr. Blifil—his conversation is so full of edification.

SOPH. (*Contemptuously*) So it would seem. I confess, however, that I am content, when I desire a sermon, to seek it in church, of a Sunday.

COPSE. Dang it all, my sentiments. One day be enough for the parson say I.

BLI. My dear Miss Western, you misunderstand me. I was merely uttering a simple moral truth—

SQUARE. (*Lugubriously*) One which I should like my other pupil, Mr. Jones, to take to heart.

SOPH. Mr. Jones is at least no hypocrite, Sir. All his faults lie upon the surface, and unfortunately, are at once detected by his *friends*.

SQUARE. I fear we have not yet got to the bottom of them.

BLI. (*Sighs significantly*)

The reviewers praised *Sophia* as they had no other play of Buchanan's. His greatest achievement, they thought, was that he had been able to convert a loose-jointed, ribald novel into a coherent and thoroughly delightful play, still preserving the essential mood and flavor of Fielding. They found it highly superior to the insipid comic operas then in vogue. The *Illustrated London News* pronounced it "the best acted and the most interesting play now to be seen in London,"[19] and the *Graphic* noted that it had been produced in New York, where it had met with equal success.[20]

In *Joseph's Sweetheart*, staged also at the Vaudeville on March 8, 1888, Buchanan used much the same adaptive technique that he had in *Sophia*. Once again he changed the story freely to suit his purpose and his public, wrote a great deal of new and dramatically effective dialogue, and pulled a rambling novel together to form a closely knit and credible play. Fielding's burlesque of *Pamela* is minimized almost to the vanishing point; Lady Booby's pursuit of Joseph is magnified almost to the degree of villainy. Lord Fellamar is transplanted from *Tom Jones* and, urged on by Lady

Booby, who hopes thus to dispose of Fanny's rivalry, pursues Fanny with the intention of making her his mistress. Parson Adams remains the lovable, comic clergyman that Fielding created, but Joseph assumes truly heroic proportions when he establishes his true identity as Mr. Wilson's son, fights a duel with Fellamar, and wounds him in revenge for that nobleman's attempts upon Fanny. All ends well when Fellamar and Slipslop expose the machinations of Lady Booby, who beats a final retreat in great discomfiture. Buchanan concludes the play with the very clever touch of having Parson Adams deliver in heroic couplets his blessing upon the soon-to-be-celebrated nuptials of Joseph and Fanny.

Joseph's Sweetheart found even greater favor with the reviewers than had *Sophia*, most of them agreeing that it was a better rendering of Fielding than the earlier play. The public seconded the critics' judgment, for the play held the boards solidly for over two years and was still being given an occasional performance late in 1891.

For his *Dick Sheridan*, produced at the Comedy Theatre on February 3, 1894, Buchanan did not have a novel to work from, but he had something equally dramatic in the stirring career of Richard Sheridan. Once again he did his materials justice, for he produced a lively, exciting play in which the dramatic interest rises steadily from its opening scene at Bath to its final curtain in London in which Sheridan proclaims that his next play will deal with his own and Miss Linley's struggle against malicious gossip and will be entitled *The School for Scandal*. The plot centers around the efforts of Sheridan and Miss Linley to defeat the machinations not only of the villainous Captain Matthews, who seeks by all kinds of foul means to get Miss Linley for himself, but also of the almost equally dastardly Lady Miller, who is enamored of Sheridan. Interwoven into this story is the struggle of Sheridan to win success as a playwright on the London stage. The action climaxes in a duel in which Sheridan worsts Captain Matthews just as the news arrives from Covent Garden that *The Rivals*, which had failed in its first performance because of the villainy of Matthews, has achieved a monumental success.

In sharp contrast was the indifferent success which greeted Buchanan's offering, despite the fact that its cast included Sir Henry Irving as Sheridan, Winifred Emory as Miss Linley, Cyril Maude as Lord Dazzleton, and Brandon Thomas as the comical

O'Leary. The reviewers blamed the failure of the play upon the writing—an accusation not borne out by a reading of the script—and upon the fact that most of the acting, even Irving's, fell into hollow stereotypes. At any rate, *Dick Sheridan* soon passed from the boards.

Following *Dick Sheridan*, Buchanan attempted only one more wholly original play, *Lady Gladys*, already discussed. Then came the disastrous *A Society Butterfly*, in collaboration with Henry Murray, which brought Buchanan to the court of bankruptcy. Thereafter he collaborated in six plays with Harriett Jay. Three of these—*The Strange Adventures of Miss Brown* (1895), *The Romance of the Shopwalker* (1896), and *The Wanderer from Venus*—contain excellent writing and exhibit a high degree of dramatic skill in handling plot and character. Unfortunately, none of them achieved real box-office success. Their last offering, *Two Little Maids from School*, appears to be nothing more than an adaptation of a French play. It also met with mediocre success and rang down the final curtain upon Buchanan's theatrical career in November, 1898.

CHAPTER 7

The Victorian Novelist

AS a novelist, Buchanan displays the same extraordinary productivity we have seen in his poems and plays. In the twenty-four years, beginning in 1876 and ending in 1900, he published twenty-five full-length novels, or better than one a year. These figures tell once again the story of writing too rapidly and too much, and they result from the same combination of unfortunate circumstances that plagued Buchanan throughout his career. He was forced into novel-writing by his ever increasing need for money to support his family, as well as by his personal follies of betting on horse races and of permitting himself to be a "soft-touch" for impecunious friends and acquaintances.

Buchanan left no written complaint against the restrictions upon the novelist as he did against those upon the playwright; but, as always, he quarreled with adverse critics here also. While publishers could and often did refuse to publish novels which they deemed offensive to the public taste, they were generally much more lenient than the theater managers or the Lord Chamberlain's Licenser of Plays. Furthermore, since Buchanan wrote all but one of his novels himself, he did not have to compromise with collaborators as he often did in the dramas. He was, therefore, freer to choose his materials and to express his own opinions. The novels, consequently, break into viable categories; and it is in these categories that I propose to discuss them: the novels of purpose, those dealing with the supernatural, the religious novels, and the "new" novels—those written after the catastrophe of 1894 that reveal a new view of life and character.

I *The Novels of Purpose*

As might be expected, the Owenite Victorian is clearly discernible in many of Buchanan's novels. Where he could do so, Buchanan used them as sounding boards for many of the social causes and views that were close to his heart. These are the same strains that reverberate throughout his poetry and some of the plays: the evils of war, the belief in the fundamental goodness of mankind, the social injustice wreaked upon woman by unequal laws and the lust of unscrupulous men, the evils of alcohol. These subjects form the basic themes of seven of the novels which are so structured as to drive home Buchanan's convictions with considerable force.

In two novels—*The Shadow of the Sword* (1876) and *That Winter Night* (1886)—Buchanan labors to expose the utter folly and the futility and barbarity of war as a curse perpetrated upon mankind in the name of patriotism by the forces of tyranny and greed. *The Shadow of the Sword* is substantially the same story which he adapted to the theater five years later in 1881. The plot was in reality nothing more than a real-life story which Buchanan had come upon during a vacation spent at Étrétat in Normandy, the tale of a young Frenchman, Rohan Gwenfern, who had so strongly hated war that he had gone to great lengths and had suffered great privations in order to avoid being conscripted into the armies of Napoleon I. The story was one with which Owenite Buchanan was bound to sympathize; moreover, since he wrote most of it during 1875, just a few years after the Franco-Prussian War, his personal reaction to the horrors of that conflict—set forth in detail in *The Drama of Kings*—strongly reinforced his Owenite antipathy to war. The result was the novel, which he serialized in the *Gentleman's Magazine* in twelve monthly installments. For the serial rights alone, Buchanan asked and presumably received one hundred and eighty guineas, not a bad price for a first novel.

The chief difference between the novel and the play is that, although the play ends with the defeat of Napoleon at Leipzig, the return of the Bourbons, and the public proclamation of Rohan's pardon just as he is about to be executed, the novel includes Napoleon's escape from Elba, which forces Rohan once more to go into hiding. Convinced that he will never have peace until he personally slays Napoleon, Rohan hides himself in the garret of a cottage in which the Emperor spends the night. But as Rohan stands with his dagger in hand, looking down at the sleeping Napoleon, he sees only the face of a weary, careworn old man who sleeps as trustfully as a child. Rohan realizes that his intended victim, bloody though he is, is also God's creature and he decides to leave him in God's hands for punishment. He escapes and returns to his hiding place. Napoleon goes to Waterloo. This scene is an effective re-sounding of the theme of "The Vision of the Man Accurst," that no man is completely evil or deserving of eternal damnation.

Of poorer quality is *That Winter Night, or, Love's Victory* (1886), the next antiwar novel, not published until a full ten years after *The Shadow of the Sword.* The basic theme is the same that Buchanan used later in his play *Lady Gladys*—antagonism between man and woman turning into true love. Here again the Franco-Prussian War furnishes the basis of the story, and the theme centers around the hatreds aroused in otherwise good people by the cruelties and barbarities of war, also an idea which Buchanan had stressed in the earlier novel. In the plot—as lively as any devotee of light fiction could wish—a young French maiden of good family is befriended by a young German officer, one of the invaders of her country. Later, when he is wounded near her home, she takes him in and nurses him in repayment for his kindness to her and also because she finds herself half in love with him.

While nursing the German, she worries about her father, who is serving in the French army, and from whom she has not heard for several weeks. Her sympathy for the German turns to violent hatred when she discovers that he has the locket and chain she had given her father and when he confesses in a delirium that he had killed her father several weeks previously in battle. Her first impulse is to take up the helpless man's sword and slay him, but religion and her father's teachings prevent her. After an inner struggle, she can even bring herself to administer the necessary medicine to save his life. This tangled situation is resolved by the reappearance of her father with the news that, though he was thought wounded beyond hope, the German Red Cross had nursed him and saved his life. All, therefore, becomes clear and comprehensible. The German had not hated her father when he shot him: he was simply carrying out his orders as a soldier. And the anonymous Frenchman who had shot the German had done it for the same reason. All were victims of the barbarity of war.

The moral is pointed up in the last scene, two years later, with the marriage of the French girl to her German lover, who has now become a French citizen. At the wedding he announces his determination to fight no more wars for any reason whatsoever. Precisely how he intended to carry out this resolution in the event that his newly adopted country declared war and asked him to serve in its forces is not discussed. Obviously, he had not expressed these sentiments to the French officials to whom he had applied for citizenship, or they would hardly have granted it.

Akin to Buchanan's sermon preached against the inanity of the
hatreds engendered by war is his impassioned plea against all
personal human hatreds which forms the theme of *God and the Man*
(1881). This is the novel, discussed in Chapter 2, which contained
his dedicatory apology to Dante Gabriel Rossetti, and which he
adapted to the stage as *Stormbeaten* in 1883. In a short preface
Buchanan makes clear that this is the second novel in a proposed
trilogy. *The Shadow of the Sword* was an attack upon the evils of
war; this one was designed to emphasize the folly of hatred between
individuals; the third, later entitled *The Martyrdom of Madeline*,
was to have as its theme "the social conspiracy against Woman-
kind."[1]

As we have noticed, Buchanan was emotionally overwrought by
the long illness and the death of his wife in November, 1881. *God
and the Man*, with its heartfelt apology to Rossetti, was the fruit of
his anguish and soul-searching. Even more notable than the apology
is the strong affirmation of belief in God and in a personal immortality with which Buchanan closes the story. Nowhere else in any
of Buchanan's writings is there so positive a statement of faith.
For the second time in his life the loss of a dear one had brought
him face to face with the great questions of life and death. The death
of his father had plunged him into despair; the parting from his wife
led him at least into a temporary hope and belief in better things
than his peering eyes had ever before been able to discern.

The novel exhibits the same faults that we noted in the play.
Its overdone melodrama and its extravagances of emotional fervor
weary the reader. The chief fault is its too-easy solution to a profound
human problem. Transporting two enemies to a new environment
will in itself hardly turn them into friends, though it is entirely
reasonable that their becoming better acquainted might do much
to improve their relationship. Conceivably, this closer acquaintance
could have happened in England as well as in the Arctic regions.

Buchanan's third social thesis, woman as the victim of man's
injustice, cruelty, and lust, was one that lay equally close to his
heart. Not only was it an Owenite credo practiced and preached
by both Buchanan's parents, but the movement for woman's rights
was a ground swell that mounted ever higher throughout the
Victorian period in both England and America. Buchanan, an
avowed proponent of the cause, overlooked no opportunities to
advance it, as we have seen in many of his poems and plays. His

first novel in this direction was the third novel of his trilogy, *The Martyrdom of Madeline* (1882), in which he makes his heroine an actress; and he attacks through her, as he had in the play *Corinne*, the age-old assumption that actresses are immoral and cannot be admitted to the better circles of society.

But the main theme is concerned with more than the plight of the actress; it portrays a social system in which formidable forces unite, almost in a conspiracy, to the great disadvantage of woman-kind. Some of these forces are the predatory male who victimizes the naïve young girl, the unequal marriage laws slanted in favor of the husband, the gossip columnists who are always eager to believe and to insinuate the worst about an actress, and the stubborn Victorian mores that gave no quarter to the fallen woman, no matter how extenuating the circumstances of her fall.

The gist of the plot is that Madeline, the heroine, a young English girl in a French boarding school, falls into the hands of the villainous French esthete, Gavrolles, who, with the hackneyed device of a fake marriage, seduces her and makes her his accomplice in crime. From her predicament, she is rescued by a kind Englishman and returned to England, where her guardian welcomes and provides for her. Since her guardian is also a playwright, through his influence she secures leading roles in his plays and soon becomes one of the leading actresses on the London stage. Unfortunately, the details of her past life become known to unscrupulous journalists and appear as insinuations in the gossip magazines. Nevertheless, she finds love and marriage with a wealthy English widower; and, leaving the stage, she settles down to a quiet married life.

Disaster strikes when the rascally Gavrolles reappears, convinces her by a bogus marriage certificate that she and he were legally married, and torments her so cruelly that she flees from home, husband, and nemesis to seek safety in anonymity. The same benevolent Englishman who had before rescued her from Gavrolles discovers the part he has played in her disappearance, follows him to France, and kills him in a duel. Returned to England, this good angel finds Madeline in a home for reformed women of the streets and restores her to her husband. Shortly afterward, she and her husband migrate to America, where, Buchanan observes—mistakenly, we must admit—"the viperous journal of the period has not yet begun to crawl."[2]

The weakness of this novel is that Madeline's "martyrdom" is not a martyrdom; her problems are the natural consequences of her own recurring folly. She runs away from the finishing school with Gavrolles not because she loves him but because of a pique she has developed against the headmistress. Again, when the rascal approaches her in England, she does not confide in her husband, whom she has fully informed of her past, but chooses to deal with the situation herself. Furthermore, completely aware of the rascality of Gavrolles as she is, she permits herself to be hoodwinked a second time by his claims of marriage and to be driven to the brink of suicide by his bogus certificate. In short, the novel is melodramatic in its plot, in its characters, and in the unrestrained quality of the writing.

The best portions of the novel are those scenes in which Buchanan satirizes the cult of estheticism; for, to point up his case, he makes his villain an esthete. These are done with a light touch and a delicious mockery that are in sharp contrast with the melodrama. In connection with the attack on estheticism is Buchanan's berating of the critics that I have discussed in Chapter 3 in relation to his two anonymous poems, *St. Abe and his Seven Wives* and *White Rose and Red*. This lampoonery, too, is cleverly done and adds considerable interest to the novel.

Buchanan's second novel about the wronged woman was *Annan Water* (1883). Published less than eighteen months after *The Martyrdom of Madeline*, this story is along parallel lines except for a few minor differences. Omitted are the attacks on the press, estheticism, and the critics. The locale is changed to Scotland; a wealthy Scottish lady turns out to be the mother of the unfortunate heroine; the French rascal this time is really married to the heroine, who has a child by him, thus complicating the situation considerably. But all turns out well in the end when the villain is slain, clearing the way for the Scottish hero to wed the heroine, who inherits a fortune from her mother.

Buchanan's third novel about the woman-victim theme was *The Heir of Linne* (1888). This narrative is also set in Scotland, but the plot varies considerably from that of *Annan Water*. The victimizer this time is the crusty old Laird of Linne, who, years before, had seduced a Scottish peasant girl and had had a son by her. Refusing to marry her, he had sent her and the baby to Canada; but news arrived that the ship had foundered, and they had been lost. An eccentric ex-clergyman of the neighborhood, Willie Macgillvray, takes the Laird to task for his sins and brings him to repentance. Part of his atonement is to adopt an orphan girl of the village and rear her as his daughter. He makes her his chief heir, but adds a clause to his will that, if the lost illegitimate son should reappear, he is to have the bulk of the estate. Of course, the son appears incognito, wins the love of the orphan, outwits a rascally nephew of the old Laird who complicates the plot, and settles down with his bride to enjoy his title and his fortune as the new Lord of Linne.

The best features of this novel are the authentic touches of Scottish life and character Buchanan works into it. Willie Macgillvray is so delightfully eccentric and yet realistic in his homely philosophy and in his pithy language that he may well have been drawn from someone Buchanan knew intimately; but, even so, the portrait is a genuine work of art. The stubborn old Laird, too, is quite convincing and original. The warm friendship of the two old men enriches an otherwise ordinary novel. In relation to Buchanan's own history it is worth noting that Willie had been one of Robert Owen's missionaries until alcohol had cost him his position. Now a confirmed teetotaler, he lectures to all who will listen on his two favorite themes of the love and reverence a son owes his mother and of the evils of drink. The two themes are associated in Willie's mind because his own alcoholism had sorely distressed his mother.

The Woman and the Man (1893) sounded once more the same theme but with the emphasis on the injustice to a woman of the marriage laws and customs. Otherwise, there are no important changes in plot, characterization, or viewpoint; for the novel is only an adaptation of his play *The Man and the Woman* of 1889. We wonder why Buchanan transposed the two nouns in the title unless it was to avoid legal action by whoever had purchased the play. The novel affords evidence of hasty writing and of the use of extraneous material, possibly to fill the requisite number of pages. Since it was published toward the end of 1893, while Buchanan's bankruptcy took place in 1894, it is probable that the book represents a desperate attempt to stave off financial disaster.

Buchanan's last venture on the woman-victim concept was *Lady Kilpatrick* (1895). Although this tale is set in Ireland with Irish characters, it employs the same plot that he had used in *The Heir of Linne*. This time, however, Moya Macartney, the wronged peasant girl, is allowed to return with her son to take her rightful place as Lady Kilpatrick. This change is accomplished by having the supposedly spurious priest who performed the supposedly fake marriage—Buchanan's usual gimmick for explaining why his heroines permit themselves to be seduced—turn out to be a real priest and the marriage to be valid. But this novel is written with such ease and charm and is so free of the inanities and absurdities that mar its four predecessors of the woman-victim theme that it lends substance to Harriett Jay's claim that Buchanan's bankruptcy was a disguised blessing which shook him out of his mad race for money and forced him to take a more realistic view of himself and the world.[3] Certain it is that there is little that is extraneous in *Lady Kilpatrick*. The plot unfolds swiftly and moves as surely to its climax and dénouement. The characters come to life with an immediacy lacking in *The Heir of Linne* except for Willie Mac-gillvary and the Laird. Best of all, the melodrama of the earlier novels is completely absent.

In both *The Heir* and *Lady Kilpatrick* Buchanan touches upon the evils of alcoholism. But in *Rachel Dene* (1895), he preaches a fervent sermon on the havoc that can be wrought in even a good man's life by drinking and gambling. Since the gambling in this case is horse-betting, we have to suspect that he was using some of his own personal experiences which resulted in bankruptcy. Buchanan's hero is a young man in a textile mill who wins the favor of the owner because he invents a machine which promises to increase profits. The owner's daughter, Rachel Dene, regards him with interest and affection. But he takes to liquor and gambling and worsens so rapidly that he is suspected and sent to prison for a murder of which he is innocent. All is solved when the real murderer confesses. The hero, who has learned his lesson, is freed. He marries Rachel and succeeds her father as owner of the mill. The weakest feature of this novel is the hero's too sudden change from virtue to drinking and gambling, a fault which originated in the impatience of Buchanan's own nature and which prevented his mastering the technique of portraying gradual developments in character. Otherwise, the novel is well written, and the characterizations are generally authentic.

The final novel of purpose, *A Child of Nature* (1881), launches a protest against the deleterious effects of English absentee land-lordism upon the Scottish Hebrides. This novel Buchanan adapted to the theater in 1887 as *The Blue Bells of Scotland*. In the novel, the English lord is not the rascally seducer that he is in the play, nor does he die in India as punishment for his sins. He lives, marries the heroine, discharges his cruel overseer, and lives in peace and amity with his tenants. This conclusion in no way solved the basic economic difficulties of the impoverished Highlanders, but it did furnish a satisfactory close for the novel.

II *Novels of the Supernatural*

Buchanan's incessant probing into the mystery of God and of death resulted in two novels dealing with the supernatural. The earliest of these was given the fanciful title of *Love Me Forever,* and it was first published in the Christmas number of *The Illustrated London News* for 1882, appearing in book form in 1883. Essentially, this book contains the same material that Buchanan cast into poetry nine years later in *The Outcast,* the story of *The Flying Dutchman* and its blasphemous Dutch captain, Philip Vanderdecken, who, enraged by his inability to round Cape Horn, calls down God's vengeance by his vain oath to keep trying until Judgment Day. And of course it is also the story of Charles Maturin's *Melmoth the Wanderer;* for, by Christ's intercession, Vanderdecken is permitted to spend one year in every seven ashore seeking a maiden whose love will free him from the curse. Buchanan achieves a happy ending to this gloomy tale by having the hero turn out to be a descendant of Vanderdecken and by having the love of the heroine inspire him to reform his life of crime and brigandage. The real Vanderdecken never appears except in a nightmarish dream of the heroine.

The central idea of *The Moment After* (1890) might well have been suggested to Buchanan by Browning's poem, "An Epistle," for it, too, deals with a man who has been dead, or nearly dead, and then has revived. Buchanan's protagonist is a man convicted of murdering his adulterous wife and her lover. When he is hanged, the rope parts slowly, strand by strand, and his body falls to the ground. Revived by the prison authorities, he insists that he has been in the other world, that he there met and became reconciled with his murdered victims, and that all three journeyed to the gates of a heavenly city where they were greeted by Christ. Just as they were about to be judged, he awoke to find himself once again on earth. He begs for the execution to continue so that he may rejoin his comrades, for he is convinced that, until he does so, they must remain outside the gates of Heaven. However, the authorities commute his sentence to life imprisonment. Shortly afterward, when he is found dead with a blissful expression on his face, the prison chaplain is certain that he has found eternal happiness, the promised happiness of his dream; but the prison physician remains skeptical. Thus Buchanan, having once again posed the question of immortality, leaves the matter just where he leaves it in his poetry— squarely on dead center.

The whole matter of the occult claims of spiritualism is examined in *The Charlatan* (1895)—nothing more than a recasting in novel form of Buchanan's play of the same title of 1894. Since the novel was a collaboration with Henry Murray, and since it shows no significant changes from the play, it needs no discussion.

III *Novels on Religious Matters*

During 1884 Buchanan published two novels which represent an attack on the Anglican Communion because they focus upon the vagaries and the frailties of two Anglican clergymen who are highly discreditable to the Establishment. The first, *The New Abelard*, appeared in March, followed by *Foxglove Manor* in September. Ambrose Bradley, the titular figure of *The New Abelard*, is a vacillating weakling who has broadened his religion to the point that he scarcely knows what he believes. His attempts to reconcile science, art, and religion cause trouble with his Bishop and lead to his resigning his living. Having fallen in love with a wealthy young parishioner, he marries her even though he has learned that his faithless first wife, whom he had long supposed dead, still lives. His bigamy is exposed, and he confesses all to his new partner. She, saddened, becomes a Roman Catholic and dies, leaving her fortune to an order of nuns. The heartbroken Bradley journeys to Oberammergau, where his faith is restored by the famous Passion Play shortly before his own death.

Foxglove Manor is even more dastardly, for the young clergyman is a liar, a lecher, and a coward named Charles Santley, a name that is possibly intended as a pun on the adjective "saintly." After seducing and nearly causing the death of his church organist, he directs his attentions to a married woman of the neighborhood, and has nearly accomplished his purpose when her husband learns of what is going on and so terrifies Santley that he leaves in frantic haste for parts unknown. Some time later, religious papers carry the news that he has entered the Church of Rome.

Of the two novels, *The New Abelard* shows the better writing, better depiction of scene and character, and more sympathetic handling of materials. *Foxglove Manor* is so marred by an improbable plot, poorly drawn characters, and so many instances of bad taste that it is a regrettable performance. Although Buchanan prefaced both stories with a disavowal that either was an attack upon the clergy, most of the reviewers were not beguiled. A few admired his courage for daring to express a negative view of the clergy, but most thought his time and talents should have been better employed.

The Rev. Annabel Lee (1898), a futuristic novel set in England of the twenty-first century, is designed to show the inadequacies of Comtean Positivism. Positivism has replaced all the old religions, and people calmly accept its dogma that all life ceases with death. But with the death of her brother in her girlhood, Annabel Lee realizes the emptiness of such doctrines. When she discovers some Christian documents of 1890, she is so inspired that she goes about England preaching the Christian gospel. A great earthquake aids her in combating Positivistic intolerance and bigotry. The novel concludes with her denunciation of Positivism and with her prophecy that Christianity will overcome all opposition. Because Buchanan was more interested in his philosophical premises than in telling a story, the novel suffers. The plot is patently designed to suit his purposes, and his characterization is equally contrived.

IV *The "New" Novels*

The new Buchanan who emerged from the financial chastening of 1894 is clearly evident in three of his very best novels—*Diana's Hunting* (1895), *Effie Hetherington* (1896), and *Father Anthony* (1898). Like *Lady Kilpatrick*, they are almost entirely free from melodramatic fustian; they reflect a deeper understanding of life and character, especially that of women; they show a restrained, refined style of writing that is in sharp and welcome contrast to Buchanan's earlier ranting; best of all, the dialogue is suited to the character and subtly reveals nuances of meaning that greatly enrich and deepen the story. All three books probe depths of life and complexities of character almost totally absent from the earlier novels. Even more remarkable is it that none of them is concerned with advancing an Owenite tenet.

Diana's Hunting deals with the predatory activities of the young actress, Diana Meredith, who stalks the playwright, Frank Horsham, with all the determination of the ancient Greek deity for whom she is named. Not at all deterred by his being married and the father of a little girl, she leaves no wile untried in her efforts to entice him away from his family; and she is only thwarted in the end by a friendly drama critic who finally brings Horsham to realize that his true happiness lies in remaining in England with his wife and child instead of following Diana to America. Diana is one aspect of the new woman, a sister to Becky Sharp, Hedda Gabbler, and Nana. In creating her, Buchanan uses throughout the novel the objective method of Ibsen. Through her deeds and her words he reveals her motivation with a crystal clarity. The other characters are very well done, but Diana is an artistic gem.

The same fundamental theme and a corresponding artistry are employed in *Effie Hetherington*—another story of the havoc wrought by a selfish, vain coquette upon the lives of others. Minor variations from *Diana's Hunting* are effected by using the love-triangle motif, with Effie pursuing the husband of another woman and turning a deaf ear to the wooing of the hero, an admirable young man who would make her an excellent husband. Psychological complexity is added by the fact that Effie's pursuit of the husband springs not from her love of the man but from a malicious desire to embarrass and wound his wife.

No better illustration could be given of what Buchanan's new artistic vision meant to his work than the third of the new works, *Father Anthony*. For this novel is only a reworking of his and G.R. Sims's collaborative play of 1890, *The English Rose,* a rather low-grade Adelphi melodrama. But with what difference, with what more profound perception, with what greater artistry is the novel written! The focus of the story is on Father Anthony Creenan, a shy, diffident young Irish priest who, on the surface, appears to be cast in the same mold as Ambrose Bradley of *The New Abelard.* Underneath, however, he is made of true steel; and he remains faithful to his priestly vows even at the cost of his own life. Equally fascinating is Father Anthony's clerical superior, Father John Croly. Genial and bibulous, he wins the affectionate friendship of his flock by his camaraderie and his good-natured raillery, while the solemnity and earnest reverence with which he conducts the rites of the church earn their respect and obedience. He casts an emollient glow over the novel, relieving, yet blending with, yet in contrast to, the tragic pathos of Father Anthony. The tender affection of the two priests for each other and their loving concern for their flock cause us to wonder if this novel could be the work of the same hand that wrote *Foxglove Manor*. The same hand, perhaps, but certainly not the same person. Buchanan had indeed changed.

Unfortunately, the change was not perceived by most of the reviewers. Buchanan's frequent potboilers, both on the stage and in his novels, had so damaged his reputation that these three excellent works received indifferent notice from the critics. The *Spector* and the *Outlook* praised the artistry and the power of *Effie Hetherington*;[4] the *Academy* thought *Diana's Hunting* "neither edifying nor amusing";[5] and the *Westminster Review* slighted *Father Anthony* as a fairly good Irish novel with an artificial plot.[6] If Buchanan could have had ten more years of high-quality work, he might have redeemed the reputation he had lost. But his life was near its end, and the opportunity was denied him.

For the sake of completeness I list here six novels that I do not intend to discuss because they are only potboilers. Their publication dates cover a span from 1885 to 1900, for even in his "new" period he did write two of them. Most of the six are hastily and poorly written; those that show better writing have such hackneyed plots and characters that they must be categorized as potboilers. Since they cannot be included in any of the classifications I have used in this chapter, I am placing them here. Their titles and publication dates are as follows: *Stormy Waters* (1885), *The Master of the Mine* (1885), *Matt. A Story of a Caravan* (1885), *Come Live with Me and Be My Love* (1891), *Marriage by Capture* (1896), and *Andromeda* (1900).

One of the very last works to come from Buchanan's hand, *Andromeda*, is of biographical interest because it depicts the agony a playwright undergoes on the first night of his play until the audience reaction finally reaches a pitch of enthusiasm that tells him he has achieved success. Of significance also is a prefatory notice to the novel warning that Buchanan reserved to himself all future dramatic rights. Clearly, his intention was to have another fling at the theater, but death prevented its fulfillment.

CHAPTER 8

The Bar of the Future

HOW then, shall we sum up the career and the contribution of Robert Williams Buchanan? Most of his contemporaries admitted that he had genius, but even his warmest friends conceded that he did not use it to its maximum potential. His besetting fault was, perhaps, that he did not love literature sufficiently to devote his energies to it. The true artist serves his art as a priest does his altar, immolating himself and all conflicting desires in a supreme effort to attain to the highest reach of his powers. His self-discipline must be stern; his patience must be great; his labor must be unstinting. Otherwise, he may do good work; he may even, here and there, do great work; but he will never attain to his utmost limits.

When Buchanan came to London in 1860, he was consumed with a desire for literary fame; but he did not realize that true and lasting literary fame results only from the combination of great genius and long labor. He was afflicted with the adolescent notion that he had but to look within himself, put on paper the inchoate ideas and tumultuous emotions he found there, and achieve greatness. His signal contribution, he thought, would be his religious poetry. He was certain that the peculiarities of his personal experience had given him something to say that would be acclaimed original, profound, and true. We have seen how mistaken he was. While he came close to greatness in his "Ballad of Judas Iscariot" and "Vision of the Man Accurst," most of his other religious verse brought him only ridicule and vituperation. Religion was a poor subject for him because he could never clarify his thinking about it. Had he but continued with his poems of the London poor and the Scottish peasantry, he would probably have written much better because he was well suited to sing of such humanitarian themes.

His second major error was thus his failure to recognize the true nature and direction of his genius. Conceivably, he might in time have discovered his fallacies and have corrected them, but the Fleshly Controversy precluded such a possibility. Not only did it raise up a host of enemies who pursued him all his life; but it convinced him that literature, as practiced in Victorian England, was a pseudo-art or a "hum-bug." If one wanted literary fame, Buchanan complained, he could win it only by suppressing his true opinions and saying what the public wanted to hear. He must never criticize such evils as war, imperialism, economic injustice, or "yellow journalism." Faced with such a dilemma, Buchanan's decision was easy. He could not turn his back upon his Owenite ideals of social improvement and his family motto of telling the truth and shaming the devil. Such ideals, rather than contemporary fame, became, at least in his own view, the altar that he chose to serve, regardless of the cost.

Of course, we cannot quarrel with his decision; he had the right to do with his life as he saw fit. Nor can we deny that the twentieth century has vindicated most of his social views. And we must honor him for standing in the vanguard of those who spoke out boldly for just but unpopular causes and aided in advancing them. We must, however, place on the debit side of his account the potboiling novels and plays, much of the splenetic criticism, and most of the shrill verse that came from his pen. We cannot fully accept his excuse that he was forced to such makeshifts in order to earn his living. His prodigality with much of the money that did come his way gives the lie to such a defense. Also, too many great artists have chosen to starve in a garret rather than to betray their art for us to permit Buchanan to escape our just censure for his opposite course. Nor could he have pleaded blindness to his own artistic faults. He wrote too much that was good not to have been aware of the tawdriness of his poorer offerings. His friend, George Bernard Shaw, accused him of taking greater pains with letters to the newspapers than with much of his creative work. Consequently, his reputation suffered damage from which it still has not recovered.

The financial disaster of 1894 jolted him into a realization of the folly of his ways and restored him, at least in part, to the paths of literary virtue. Had he lived longer he might have been able to win his way back to literary respectability. But the stroke of October, 1900, ended his career. We must, therefore, estimate his contribution to English literature and his rightful place in it on the basis of what he had actually accomplished.

With characteristic Owenite optimism, Buchanan prophesied that sometime in the future a new day would dawn in which the social evils he had combated would be corrected. He was confident that in that halcyon day his case would be reviewed at "the Bar of

152   ROBERT W. BUCHANAN

the Future," and that he would receive the honor that was his due, the honor that his own corrupt times had denied him. Apparently he believed that the social rightness of his views would earn for him and his works a high place. As he had done in much of his criticism of other literary figures, he failed to differentiate between social value and literary artistry. Of course, he was mistaken. While there have been a few instances in which books have risen to prominence because of social or political value, they have not been deemed great literature unless they also possessed superior literary artistry. No one, for instance, would today judge Harriett Beecher Stowe's *Uncle Tom's Cabin* to be a literary masterpiece. And Charles Dickens survives not because of the social protest in his novels but because of the literary magic with which he invested them. So far, Buchanan has not fared well. The last edition of his poetry appeared in 1901; very few of his plays have ever been published; his novels are available only in Victorian editions; only his article and his book against Dante Rossetti survive of his criticism.

Yet Buchanan deserves a better fate than oblivion. He left enough good poetry to make a respectable book; at least three of his plays—*Sophia, Joseph's Sweetheart,* and *Dick Sheridan*—deserve printing and perhaps staging; and not fewer than five of his novels— *The Shadow of the Sword, The Martyrdom of Madeline, Effie Hetherington, Diana's Hunting,* and *Father Anthony*—are too good to be forgotten. Likewise his critical essays on Swinburne and Dante Rossetti, on David Gray, on George Eliot, on the Victorian theater, Rudyard Kipling, on Walt Whitman, and his protest against Victorian criticism in "My First Books" were all of sufficient importance in their own day and they contribute so much to our understanding of the Victorian literary scene that they should be brought to the attention of modern readers. I have elsewhere mentioned Buchanan's contribution to Thomas Hardy's *The Dynasts* and possibly also to such of his novels as *Jude the Obscure* and *Tess of the D'Urbervilles;* I have also discussed the likelihood of his preparing the way for Shaw's *Widower's Houses* and *Mrs. Warren's Profession.* Neither Shaw nor Hardy ever acknowledged any indebtedness to Buchanan, an omission which would not at all have concerned Buchanan because of his philosophy that all literature was a sort of Owenite common domain from which each littérateur was free to borrow as he wished.

Stormy, contentious, irrepressible Buchanan did influence the thought and the literature of his own day and, although indirectly, of the twentieth century also. He is a Victorian figure of too much importance and interest to be relegated to literary shadow land. It is to be hoped that the final verdict from his "Bar of the Future" will yet grant him his due.

Notes and References

Chapter One

1. "Mr. Robert Buchanan," *The Times* (London), June 11, 1901, p. 7.
2. Harriett Jay, *Robert Buchanan* (London, 1903), p. 3.
3. Robert Buchanan, *Complete Poetical Works* (London, 1901), II, 276; hereafter designated as *Poetical Works*.
4. For this summary of Owen's career I have drawn upon the following works: Frank Podmore, *Robert Owen; a Biography*, 2 vols., (New York, 1907); Margaret Cole, *Robert Owen of New Lanark*, (New York, 1953); A. L. Morton, *The Life and Ideas of Robert Owen*, (London, 1962); Robert Owen, *The Life of Robert Owen*, (New York, 1920); and Robert Dale Owen, *Threading My Way*, (London, 1874).
5. Jay, p. 3.
6. *The New Moral World*, January 29, 1842, pp. 47–48.
7. Jay, p. 1.
8. *Ibid.*, p. 18.
9. *Ibid.*, pp. 15–16.
10. Genesis 16; 12. "My First Books," *Idler*, III (1893), 387.
11. "My First Books," *Idler*, III (1893), 387.
12. Jay, p. 106.
13. *Ibid.*, p. 57.
14. "My First Books," *Idler*, III (1893), 385.
15. Jay, pp. 91, 100. Buchanan, *Undertones* (London, 1865), p. 233.
16. Jay, pp. 106–107.
17. Jay, p. 242.
18. *Ibid.*, p. 290.

Chapter Two

1. *Poetical Works*, II, 276.
2. T. Hall Caine, *Recollections of Dante Gabriel Rossetti* (Boston, 1883), n. to p. 71.
3. Cecil Y. Lang, ed., *The Swinburne Letters* (New Haven, 1959–62), I, 146; hereafter designated as *Swinburne Letters*.
4. *Athenaeum* (August 4, 1866), pp. 137–38. None of the bound volumes of the *Athenaeum* that I have seen include volume numbers; hence, I have had recourse to the dates of the issues.
5. Caliban, "The Session of the Poets," *Spectator* (September 15, 1866), p. 1028.

6. *Swinburne Letters*, I, 169, 195, 200–201.

7. William Rossetti, *Dante Gabriel Rossetti, His Family Letters with a Memoir* (London, 1895), I, 295.

8. A. C. Swinburne, *Notes on Poems and Reviews* (London, 1866), pp. 5–6.

9. Thomas J. Wise, ed., *The Complete Works of Algernon Charles Swinburne* (London, 1925), XVI, 430.

10. William M. Rossetti, *Swinburne's Poems and Ballads* (London, 1866), p. 7.

11. *Athenaeum* (November 3, 1866), pp. 564–65.

12. A. C. Swinburne, "Mr. Arnold's New Poems," *Fortnightly Review*, II (October 1, 1867), 428.

13. A. C. Swinburne, "Matthew Arnold's New Poems," *Essays and Studies* (London, 1888), footnote to p. 153.

14. *Athenaeum* (January 29, 1870), pp. 154–56.

15. *Blackwood's Magazine*, CVIII (August, 1870), 178–83.

16. *North American Review*, CXI (October, 1870), 471–80. This review is unsigned, but Lang, *Swinburne Letters*, I, 194, says Lowell was the author.

17. Robert Maitland, "The Fleshly School of Poetry: Mr. D. G. Rossetti," *The Contemporary Review*, XVIII (October, 1871), 335.

18. *Ibid.*, p. 337.

19. *Ibid.*

20. *Ibid.*, p. 350.

21. *Ibid.*, p. 343.

22. *Ibid.*, p. 338.

23. *Swinburne Letters*, II, 161.

24. Sidney Colvin, *Athenaeum* (December 9, 1871), p. 755.

25. Robert Buchanan, Strahan and Company, *Athenaeum* (December 16, 1871), p. 794.

26. *Ibid.*, pp. 792–94.

27. *The Fleshly School of Poetry and Other Phenomena of the Day* (London, 1872), p. v.

28. *Ibid.*, p. 64.

29. *Ibid.*

30. *Ibid.*, p. 83.

31. *Ibid.*, p. 84.

32. *Ibid.*, pp. 85–87.

33. *Athenaeum* (May 25, 1872), pp. 650–51.

34. "Mr. Buchanan and the Fleshly Poets," *Saturday Review*, XXXIII, 700–701.

35. *Graphic*, V, 606.

36. Caine, *Recollections of Dante Gabriel Rossetti*, n. to p. 71.

37. Robert Buchanan, "The Monkey and the Microscope," *St. Paul's Magazine*, XI (August, 1872), 240.

38. A. C. Swinburne, "Epitaph on a Slanderer," *Examiner* (November 20, 1875), p. 1304.

39. Edmund Gosse and Thomas J. Wise, eds., *The Complete Works of Algernon Charles Swinburne* (London, 1926), XVIII, 260.

40. "Buchanan v. Taylor," *The Times* (London), July 3, 1876, p. 13.

41. Oswald Doughty, *Dante Gabriel Rossetti* (New Haven, 1949), p. 400.

42. "My First Books," *Idler,* III (1893), 385–96.

43. "The Gospel According to the Printer's Devil," *A Look Round Literature* (London, 1887), p. 331.

44. *Master-Spirits* (London, 1873), p. 126.

45. *Ibid.,* pp. 126–27.

46. *A Look Round Literature,* pp. 332–33.

47. *The Coming Terror* (London, 1891), p. 381.

48. *Ibid.,* pp. 8–9.

49. *Ibid.,* p. 341.

50. *Ibid.,* p. 379.

Chapter Three

1. "Prefatory Notice," *Poems of the Honorable Roden Noel* (London, [1884]), p. xxiii.

2. *David Gray and Other Essays, Chiefly on Poetry* (London, 1868), p. v.

3. *Ibid.,* p. vi.

4. *Ibid.,* p. 215.

5. *Ibid.,* p. 290–91.

6. *Athenaeum* (February 15, 1868), pp. 244–45. *Contemporary Review,* VII (1868), 470–72.

7. *St. Abe and His Seven Wives* (London, 1896); see "Bibliographical Note" following the poem.

8. Jay, p. 165.

9. *St. Abe,* p. 3.

10. *Athenaeum* (November 25, 1871), pp. 682–83.

11. *Academy,* III (January 1, 1872), 4–6.

12. *London Quarterly,* XXXVIII (1872), 258–60.

13. *Graphic,* V (January 13, 1872), 35.

14. *British Quarterly,* LV (1872), 138–39.

15. *Athenaeum* (December 23, 1871), pp. 830–831.

16. *London Quarterly,* XXXVIII (1872), 264.

17. *British Quarterly,* LV (April, 1872), 300.

18. *Graphic,* V (January 13, 1872), 35.

19. *Temple Bar,* XXXV (April, 1872), 118–19.

20. *Westminster Review* (October, 1873), p. 247.

21. Archibald Stodart-Walker, *Robert Buchanan, the Poet of Modern Revolt; an Introduction to His Poetry* (London, 1901), p. 112.

22. *A Look Round Literature*, pp. 359, 360, 382.

23. *Ibid.*, p. 385.

24. *The Coming Terror*, p. 383.

25. "My First Books," *The Idler*, III (1893), 385–96.

26. Jerome K. Jerome, ed., *My First Book* (London, 1897).

Chapter Four

1. *Academy*, LXI (October 26, 1901), 384.

2. Jay, pp. 114–15.

3. *Poetical Works*, I, 21.

4. *Ibid.*, 24.

5. *British Quarterly Review*, XXXIX (January 1, 1864), 249.

6. R. Williams Buchanan, "Merlin and the White Death," *Once A Week*, X (February 20, 1864), 251–52.

7. *Poetical Works*, I, 8–9.

8. *Ibid.*, 76.

9. *Ibid.*, 90.

10. *Ibid.*, 529.

11. *Ibid.*, 186.

12. *Ibid.*, 124.

13. *The Drama of Kings* (London, 1871), p. 465.

14. See J. Cassidy, "The Original Form of Hardy's *Dynasts*," *Publications of the Modern Language Association*, LXIX (December, 1954), 1085–1100.

15. *Poetical Works*, I, 335.

16. *The New Rome* (London, 1899), p. 385.

17. *Poetical Works*, II, 310.

18. *Academy*, LVI (January 28, 1899), 119.

19. *Poetical Works*, II, 387.

20. *Ibid.*, 402.

21. *Ibid.*, 403.

22. *Ibid.*

23. *Ibid.*, 432.

Chapter Five

1. Hoxie N. Fairchild, *Religious Trends in English Poetry* (New York, 1957), IV, 217.

2. *Poetical Works*, I, 257.

3. *Ibid.*, 287.

4. Jay, p. 140.

5. *Poetical Works*, I, 294.

6. *Athenaeum* (May 28, 1870), p. 701.

7. *London Quarterly Review*, XXXIV (1870), 525.

8. *Westminster Review*, XCIV (July, 1870), 107.

9. *North British Review*, LII (1870), 596–98.

10. *Poetical Works*, I, 492.

11. *Ibid.*, 427.

12. Jay, p. 209

13. *Illustrated London News*, LXX (March 10, 1877), 227.

14. *Academy*, XII (October 20, 1877), 382.

15. *Poetical Works*, I, 495.

16. *Ibid.*, 496.

17. Lafcadio Hearn, *Appreciations of Poetry* (New York, 1916), p. 360.

18. *The City of Dream* (London, 1888), p. 363.

19. *Poetical Works*, II, 53.

20. *Ibid.*, 63.

21. *Ibid.*, 126.

22. *Ibid.*, 134.

23. *Ibid.*, 151.

24. *Ibid.*, 160.

25. *Graphic*, XXXVII (April 21, 1888), 430.

26. Jay, p. 228.

27. *Poetical Works*, II, 168.

28. *Ibid.*, 237.

29. *Ibid.*, 242.

30. *Ibid.*, 288.

31. *Ibid.*, 294

32. *Ibid.*

33. *Ibid.*, 382.

Chapter Six

1. Allardyce Nicoll, *Late Nineteenth Century Drama*, vol. V in *A History of English Drama, 1660–1900* (Cambridge, 1962), 284–85.

2. See Buchanan's "The Modern Stage" in *A Look Round Literature* (1887), 239–302. See his *The Coming Terror* (1891) for his "The Courtesan on the Stage," 354–57; his "Dramatic Criticism as She Is Wrote," 358–60. See also his articles, "The Ethics of Play Licensing," *The Theatre*, n.s. XXVII (May, 1896), 254–57; "An Interesting Experiment," *The Theatre*, n.s. XXVIII (July, 1896), 9–11; "A Word on the Defunct Drama," *The Theatre*, n.s. XXVIII (October, 1896), 208–10.

3. G. R. Sims, *Sixty Years' Recollections of Bohemian London* (London, 1917), pp. 203–4.

4. "The Courtesan on the Stage," *The Coming Terror*, p. 355.

5. "The Modern Stage," *A Look Round Literature*, p. 294.

6. "A Word on the Defunct Drama," *The Theatre*, n.s. XXVIII (October, 1896), 208.

7. *Ibid.,* 210.

8. George Bernard Shaw, *The Complete Works of George Bernard Shaw* (New York, 1931), XXIV, 164.

9. Unless otherwise noted, all the production dates of Buchanan's plays are those given by Nicoll, *op. cit.,* pp. 284–85.

10. Jay, p. 98.

11. *Ibid.,* p. 233.

12. *Illustrated London News,* LXIX (July 1, 1876), 23.

13. Sims, p. 208.

14. *A Look Round Literature,* p. 295.

15. Jay, pp. 226–27.

16. *Ibid.,* p. 254.

17. *Athenaeum* (May 24, 1890), p. 683.

18. A note in the novel *The Charlatan* (1895), written in collaboration with Henry Murray, suggests that the two men had collaborated in the play also. But since the Lord Chamberlain ascribes the play solely to Buchanan, and since it preceded the novel by a year, I am including it among his original works.

19. *Illustrated London News,* XC (April 16, 1887), 436.

20. Under "Theatres," *Graphic,* XXXIV (November 27, 1886), 570.

Chapter Seven

1. Buchanan, *God and the Man* (London, 1883), p. iii.

2. Buchanan, *The Matyrdom of Madeline* (London, 1884), p. 200.

3. Jay, pp. 248–49.

4. *Outlook,* I (June 18, 1898), 630. *Spectator,* LXXVI (June 27, 1896), 927–28.

5. *Academy,* XLVIII (December 28, 1895), 564.

6. *Westminster Review,* CL (December, 1898), 713.

Selected Bibliography

PRIMARY SOURCES

There is no complete collection of Buchanan's works. Most of the poetry is included in *The Complete Poetical Works* of 1901, but several of the early poems are omitted from this edition; and *The Drama of Kings* is cut considerably from the original version of 1871. Of the fifty plays listed by Allardyce Nicoll in his *Late Nineteenth Century Drama* (282–83), only three have been published; and my efforts have unearthed only forty-four plays in manuscript or typescript in the Lord Chancellor's collection now in the British Museum.

None of the novels has been collected; but, since they ran through several editions in both Britain and the United States, they are not difficult to find. The same thing can be said of the volumes of criticism, which, because of their literary interest, have found their way into the libraries of most large American universities.

Although Buchanan was a prolific letter writer and carried on an extensive correspondence with a large number of important and interesting Victorians, no collection of his letters exists. Harriett Jay includes a few in her biography, as well as a few scattered excerpts from his diary, but my advertisements for such personalia both in Britain and the Unites States have met with scant success.

1. Collected Editions

Complete Poetical Works. 2 vols. London: Chatto and Windus, 1901.
The Poetical Works. 3 vols. Boston: James R. Osgood and Co., 1874.
The Poetical Works. 2 vols. London: Chatto and Windus, 1884.
Selected Poems. London: Chatto and Windus, 1882.

2. Books of Poetry

Undertones. London: Chatto and Windus, 1863.
Idylls and Legends of Inverburn. London: Alexander Strahan, 1865.
London Poems. London: Alexander Strahan, 1866.
Ballad Stories of the Affections. London: George Routledge and sons, 1866.
North Coast and Other Poems. London: George Routledge and Sons, 1867.

160

The Book of Orm. London: Chatto and Windus, 1870.
Napoleon Fallen. London: Strahan and Company, 1870.
The Drama of Kings. London: Strahan and Company, 1871.
Saint Abe and His Seven Wives. London: Strahan and Company, 1872.
White Rose and Red. London: Strahan and Company, 1873.
Balder the Beautiful. London: William Mullan and Son, 1877.
Ballads of Life, Love, and Humour. London: Chatto and Windus, 1882.
The Earthquake. London: Chatto and Windus, 1885.
The City of Dream. London: Chatto and Windus, 1888.
The Outcast. London: Chatto and Windus, 1891.
The Buchanan Ballads Old and New. London: John Haddon and Company, 1892.
The Wandering Jew. London: Chatto and Windus, 1893.
The Devil's Case. London: Robert Buchanan, 1896.
The Ballad of Mary, the Mother. London: Robert Buchanan, 1897.
The New Rome. London: Walter Scott, Ltd., 1898.

3. Novels

The Shadow of the Sword. 3 vols. London: Richard Bentley and Son, 1876.
A Child of Nature. 3 vols. London: Richard Bentley and Son, 1881.
God and The Man. London: Chatto and Windus, 1881.
The Martyrdom of Madeline. 3 vols. London: Chatto and Windus, 1882.
Love Me For Ever. London: Chatto and Windus, 1883.
Annan Water. 3 vols. London: Chatto and Windus, 1883.
Foxglove Manor. 3 vols. London: Chatto and Windus, 1884.
The New Abelard. 3 vols. London: Chatto and Windus, 1884.
The Master of the Mine. 2 vols. London: Richard Bentley and Son, 1885.
Matt. The Story of a Caravan. London: Chatto and Windus, 1885.
Stormy Waters. 3 vols. London: John and Robert Maxwell, 1885.
That Winter Night. Bristol: Arrowsmith's Bristol Library, 1886.
The Heir of Linne. 2 vols. London: Chatto and Windus, 1888.
The Moment After. London: William Heinemann, 1890.
Come Live with Me and Be My Love. London: William Heinemann, 1891.
The Woman and the Man. London: Chatto and Windus, 1893.
Rachel Dene. 2 vols. London: Chatto and Windus, 1894.
Lady Kilpatrick. London: Chatto and Windus, 1894.
The Charlatan. In collaboration with Henry Murray. London: Chatto and Windus, 1895.
Diana's Hunting. London: R. Fisher Unwin, 1895.
A Marriage by Capture. London: R. Fisher Unwin, 1896.
Effie Hetherington. London: R. Fisher Unwin, 1896.
Father Anthony. London: John Lang, 1898.
The Rev. Annabel Lee. London: C. Arthur Pearson, Ltd. 1898.
Andromeda. London: Chatto and Windus, 1900.

4. Essays

David Gray and other Essays. London: Sampson Low, Son, and Marston, 1868.
The Land of Lorne. 2 vols. London: Chapman and Hall, 1871.
The Fleshly School of Poetry and Other Phenomena of the Day. London: Strahan and Company, 1872.
Master-Spirits. London: Henry S. King and Company, 1873.
The Hebrid Isles. London: Chatto and Windus, 1882.
A Poet's Sketch-Book. London: Chatto and Windus, 1883.
A Look Round Literature. London: Ward and Downey, 1887.
On Descending into Hell. London: George Redway, 1889.
The Coming Terror. London: William Heinemann, 1891.

5. Significant Contributions to Periodicals

"A Heart Struggle. A Tale in Two Parts," Part I, *Temple Bar,* IV (December, 1861), 137–50; Part II (January, 1862), 195–215.
"Lady Letitia's Lilliput Hand," Part I, *Temple Bar,* IV (March, 1862), 551–79; Part II, V (April, 1862), 114–31.
"Wintering at Etrétat," Part I, *Argosy,* I (February, 1866), 165–72; Part II, (April, 1866), 315–24.

Review of Swinburne's *Poems and Ballads, Athenaeum* (August 4, 1866), pp. 137–38.
"The Session of the Poets," *Spectator,* XXXIX (September 15, 1866), 1028.
"Immorality in Authorship," *Fortnightly,* VI (September 15, 1866), 289–300.
"Walt Whitman," *Broadway,* I (1867–68), 188–95.
"Mr. John Morley's Essays," *Contemporary Review,* XVII (June, 1871), 319–37.
"The Fleshly School of Poetry: Mr. D. G. Rossetti," *Contemporary Review,* XVII (October, 1871), 334–50.
"The Stealthy School of Criticism," [a letter] *Athenaeum* (December 30, 1871), p. 887.
"Tennyson's Charm," *St. Paul's Magazine,* X (March, 1872), 282–303.
"The Monkey and the Microscope," *St. Paul's Magazine,* XI (August, 1872), 240.
"The Newest Thing in Journalism," *Contemporary Review,* XXX (September, 1877), 678–703.
"The Modern Drama and Its Minor Critics," *Contemporary Review,* LVI (December, 1889), 908–25.
"The Heir: a Dramatic Sketch in Four Chapters," *National Graphic,* L (December, 1894), 17–20.

"The Voice of 'The Hooligan,' " *Contemporary Review*, LXXVI (December, 1899), 776–89.

6. The Dramas

The Rathboys. In collaboration with Charles Gibbon. 1862.
The Witch Finder. 1864.
A Madcap Prince. 1874.
Corinne. 1876.
The Nine Days' Queen. 1880.
The Exiles of Erin. 1881.
The Shadow of the Sword. 1881.
Lucy Brandon. 1882.
Stormbeaten. 1883.
Lady Clare. 1883.
A Sailor and His Lass. In collaboration with Sir Augustus Harris. 1883.
Bachelors. In collaboration with H. Vezin. 1884.
Alone in London. In collaboration with Harriett Jay. 1885.
Agnes. 1885.
Sophia. 1886.
A Dark Night's Bridal. 1887.
The Queen of Connaught. 1887.
The Blue Bells of Scotland. 1887.
Fascination. In collaboration with Harriett Jay. 1887.
Partners. 1888.
Joseph's Sweetheart. 1888.
Roger-la-Honte. 1888.
That Doctor Cupid. 1889.
The Old Home. 1889.
Theodora. 1889.
The Man and the Woman. 1889.
Miss Tomboy. 1890.
The Bride of Love. 1890.
Clarissa. 1890.
Sweet Nancy. 1890.
The English Rose. In collaboration with G. R. Sims. 1890.
The Struggle for Life. In collaboration with Frederick Horner. 1890.
The Sixth Commandment. 1890.
Marmion. 1891.
The Gifted Lady. 1891
The Roll of the Drum. In collaboration with G. R. Sims. 1891.
The White Rose. In collaboration with G. R. Sims. 1892.
The Lights of Home. In collaboration with G. R. Sims. 1892.
The Black Domino. In collaboration with G. R. Sims. 1893.

The Pied Piper of Hamelin. 1893. Music by F. W. Allwood.
The Charlatan. 1894.
Dick Sheridan. 1894.
Lady Gladys. 1894.
A Society Butterfly. In collaboration with Henry Murray. 1894.
The Strange Adventures of Miss Brown. In collaboration with Harriett Jay. 1895.
The New Don Quixote. In collaboration with Harriett Jay. 1896.
The Romance of the Shopwalker. In collaboration with Harriett Jay. 1896.
The Wanderer from Venus. In collaboration with Harriett Jay. 1896.
The Mariners of England. In collaboration with Harriett Jay. 1897.
Two Little Maids from School. In collaboration with Harriett Jay. 1898.

SECONDARY SOURCES

1. Bibliographical

BATESON, F. W. *The Cambridge Bibliography of English Literature*. III, New York: The Macmillan Company, 1941. By no means a complete bibliography.
JAY, HARRIETT. *Robert Buchanan*. London: T. Fisher Unwin, 1903. Miss Jay gives a partial bibliography of Buchanan's writings (316–19). I have found some errors in her dates of publication.

2. Critical and Biographical

BESANT, WALTER. "Is It the Voice of the Hooligan?" *Contemporary Review*, LXXVII (January, 1900), 27–39. Reply to Buchanan's attack upon Kipling.
CASSIDY, JOHN A. "Robert Buchanan and the Fleshly Controversy," *Publications of the Modern Language Association*, LXVII (March, 1952), 65–93.
————. "The Original Source of Hardy's *Dynasts*," *Publications of the Modern Language Association*, LXIX (December, 1954), 1085–1100.
COLE, JOHN W. *The Life and Theatrical Times of Charles Kean, F.S.A.* 2 vols. London: Richard Bentley, 1859. Contains much information about the Victorian theater.
COLE, MARGARET. *Robert Owen of New Lanark*. New York: Oxford University Press, 1953. Good account of Owen's social experiments at New Lanark.
FAIRCHILD, HOXIE N. "The Immediate Source of *The Dynasts*," *Publications of the Modern Language Association*, LXVII (March, 1952), 43–64. Shows that Hardy borrowed importantly from Buchanan's *Drama of Kings* for *The Dynasts*.
————. "Buchanan and Noel." *Religious Trends in English Poetry*. IV.

New York: Columbia University Press, 1957. Compares the poetry of Buchanan and Roden Noel, generally to Buchanan's disfavor.

HEARN, LAFCADIO. *Appreciations of Poetry.* New York: Dodd, Mead and Company, 1916. Critical estimate of Buchanan's work by a noted critic of the twentieth century.

HYDER, C. K. *Swinburne Replies.* Syracuse University Press, 1966. Brief, scholarly account of some of Swinburne's polemics, together with reprints of *Notes on Poems and Reviews* and *Under the Microscope.*

JAY, HARRIETT. *Robert Buchanan.* London: T. Fisher Unwin, 1903. A "family" biography, but gives much firsthand information about Buchanan.

LANG, CECIL Y. ed. *The Swinburne Letters.* 6 vols. New Haven: Yale University Press, 1959–62. Indispensable; gives Swinburne's reactions to Buchanan.

MORDELL, ALBERT. *Notorious Literary Attacks.* New York: Bonie and Liveright, 1926. Contains an account of the Fleshly Controversy.

MORTON, A. L. *The Life and Ideas of Robert Owen.* London: Lawrence and Wishart, 1962. Good recent analysis.

MURRAY, HENRY. *Robert Buchanan. A Critical Appreciation.* London: Philip Welby, 1901. Criticism by a friend and literary associate of Buchanan.

NICOLL, ALLARDYCE. *Late Nineteenth Century Drama,* vol. V in *A History of English Drama,* 1660–1900. Cambridge: Cambridge University Press, 1962.

NOBLE, JAMES A. "Robert Buchanan." *The Poets and the Poetry of the Century.* VI. London: Hutchinson and Company, [1896] 517–26. Victorian criticism of Buchanan's poetry.

NOEL, RODEN. "Robert Buchanan." *Essays on Poetry and Poets.* London: Kegan Paul, Trench and Company, 1886. Appreciative criticism by a close friend of Buchanan.

OWEN, ROBERT. *The Life of Robert Owen.* New York: Alfred A. Knopf, 1920. Owen's autobiography.

OWEN, ROBERT DALE. *Threading My Way.* London: Turner and Company, 1874. Contains view of Owen by his son.

PODMORE, FRANK. *Robert Owen: A Biography.* 2 vols. New York: D. Appleton and Company, 1907. The definitive biography of Robert Owen; indispensable.

SHAW, G. B. *The Collected Works of George Bernard Shaw.* 30 vols. Ayot St. Lawrence Edition. New York: Wm. Wise, 1930–32. Vols. XXIII, XXIV, and XXV contain incidental criticism of Buchanan's plays during the 1890's.

SIMS, G. R. *Sixty Years' Recollections of Bohemian London.* London: Eveleigh Nash Company, Ltd., 1917. Reminiscences of Buchanan in the theater by a friend and collaborator.

SMITH, GEORGE BARNETT. "Robert Buchanan," *Contemporary Review*, XXII (1873), 872–902. Eulogy of Buchanan by one of his friends.

STODART-WALKER, ARCHIBALD. *Robert Buchanan, the Poet of Modern Revolt*. London: Grant Richards, 1901. A summing-up of Buchanan's literary career and works by a friendly critic.

STOREY, GEORGE G. "Robert Buchanan's Critical Principles," *Publications of the Modern Language Association*, LXVIII, 1228–32. Professor Storey traces Buchanan's critical principles to those of Goethe and argues that they underlay his personal differences with the Pre-Raphaelites and led to the Fleshly Controversy.

SWINBURNE, ALGERNON C. *Under the Microscope*. London: D. White, 1872. Swinburne's rejoinder to Buchanan's attack upon him and Rossetti in the Fleshly School article in the *Contemporary Review* in October, 1871.

SYMONS, ARTHUR. "Robert Buchanan." *Studies in Prose and Verse*. London: J. M. Dent and Company, 1904. Derogatory view of Buchanan by a young critic sympathetic to the Rossettis.

WATSON, ERNEST B. *Sheridan to Robertson*. New York: Benjamin Blom, Inc., 1926. Excellent history of the nineteenth-century British theater.

Index

Essays and Reviews (Cont.)
Thing in Journalism," 59; "A Note on Dante Rossetti," 57; review of Swinburne's *Notes on Poems and Reviews,* 41; review of Swinburne's *Poems and Ballads,* 39, 41; review of William Rossetti's edition of Shelley, 42; "The Voice of the Hooligan," 60
Novels:
   Andromeda, 149; *Annan Water,* 142; *The Charlatan,* 146; *The Child of Nature,* 127, 144; *Come Live with Me and Be My Love,* 149; *Diana's Hunting,* 147–148, 149, 152; *Effie Hetherington,* 147–148, 149, 152; *Father Anthony,* 147–149, 152; *Foxglove Manor,* 146–147, 149; *God and Man,* 56, 125, 140; *The Heir of Linne,* 142, 144; *Lady Kilpatrick,* 143–144; *Love Me Forever,* 145; *Marriage by Capture,* 149; *The Martyrdom of Madeline,* 59, 74, 128, 141–142, 152; *The Master of the Mine,* 149; *Matt. A Story of a Caravan,* 149; *The Moment After,* 145–146; *The New Abelard,* 146, 147, 148; *Rachel Dene,* 144; *The Rev. Annabel Lee,* 147; *The Shadow of the Sword,* 33, 138, 152; *Stormy Waters,* 149; *That Winter's Night,* 138, 139; *The Woman and the Man,* 143
Plays:
   Alone in London, 32, 121, 126, 127, 128, 130; *The Blue Bells of Scotland,* 127–128, 144; *The Bride of Love,* 130; *The Charlatan,* 130–131, 146; *Corinne,* 33, 124–125, 141; *Dick Sheridan,* 135–136, 152; *The English Rose,* 148; *Joseph's Sweetheart,* 121, 135, 152; *Lady Gladys,* 131, 136, 139; *The Madcap Prince,* 33, 124; *The Man and the Woman,* 128–130, 143; *Marmion,* 121; *The Old Home,* 128; *The Pied Piper of Hamelin,* 121; *The Rathboys,* 27, 121; *The Romance of the Shopwalker,* 136; *The Shadow of the Sword,* 125; *A Social Butterfly,* 33, 136; *Sophia,* 121, 132, 134, 152; *Stormbeaten,* 125;

Plays (Cont.)
   The Strange Adventures of Miss Brown, 136; *Two Little Maids from School,* 121, 136; *The Wanderer from Venus,* 123, 136; *The Witchfinder,* 27, 124, 125
Poems:
   Balder the Beautiful, 103–105; "The Ballad of Judas Iscariot," 105–106, 114, 117, 122, 150; *The Ballad of Mary the Mother,* 115, 118–119; *The Book of Orm,* 82, 97, 99–103, 104, 105, 108, 115; *The City of Dream,* 34, 99, 108–114, 115, 122; *Complete Poetical Works,* 80, 84, 93, 96; "The Dead," 28; "The Dead Baby," 28; "The Destitute," 28; *The Devil's Case,* 89, 115–116; *The Drama of Kings,* 70, 72, 73, 76, 80, 88, 91–93, 138; *The Earthquake,* 106–108; "Fra Giacomo," 82; *Idylls and Legends of Inverburn,* 82, 85, 86; *London Poems,* 82, 88; "The Monkey and the Microscope," 55; *Napoleon Fallen,* 91, 108; *The New Rome,* 32, 88, 93, 94, 96, 97, 115, 119; *North Coast and Other Poems,* 85; *The Outcast,* 115, 116–117, 145; "The Outcasts," 28; *Poetical Works* (1874), 105–106; *St. Abe and His Seven Wives,* 70–73, 74, 75, 77, 80, 142; "The Session of the Poets," 40, 47, 55, 56, "Socrates in Camden," 32; *Undertones,* 27, 82, 83; "Walt Whitman," 32; *The Wandering Jew,* 34, 115, 117–118; *White Rose and Red,* 54, 73–74, 75, 77, 80, 142
Bunyan, John, 108
Burns Birthday Dinner, 95
Burns, Robert, 59, 81, 85, 86, 87, 95
Byron, Lord, 116, 117

Caine, Hall, 57, 78
Caledonian Club, 95
Caliban, 40
Canton, William, 105
Carlyle, Thomas, 15, 36, 59, 60, 68, 94, 107, 116

89894